IN A FOG

· · · · · · · · · · · · · · · · ·

THE HUMORISTS' GUIDE TO ENGLAND

Edited by

Robert Wechsler

ROBERT HALE · LONDON

ISBN 0-7090-4806-8 (*hardback*)
ISBN 0-7090-4781-9 (*paperback*)

Robert Hale Limited
Clerkenwell House
Clerkenwell Green
London EC1R 0HT

Printed in Great Britain by
St Edmundsbury Press Limited, Bury St Edmunds, Suffolk
and bound by WBC Bookbinders Ltd, Bridgend, Glamorgan

IN A FOG

Robert Wechsler is a well-known American publisher and editor who has created a series of humorous guides to France, Italy, the USA and to the ocean cruise.

CONTENTS

*"Pardon me, we're from New Orleans—
would you call this foggy?"*

TRAVEL GUIDES ARE WHAT YOU READ when you want to know where to stay and what to see and where to eat and what to do about such things as customs and transportation and shopping. This is not that sort of guide.

Humorists don't care whether you want to rent a castle or go from one bed-and-breakfast to another; they know that however you go, you'll squabble about the bathroom (too ancient or too many children in it at all hours of the day and night), and whether this or that is quaint or modern enough (if only more of England could be both, rather than neither!).

So forget everything you've ever thought about guidebooks. The advice here is much simpler: relax and enjoy. Remember: it's your holiday, so don't annoy yourself about the prices or the service or driving on the left side of the road. Well, if you have to worry about something, go ahead and worry about driving on the left side of the road, just don't practice anywhere else.

Although we go to England to see the Charleses and Dis, what we see more of, and what humorists can never get enough of, are the Jonathans and Reginalds, the Margarets and Amelias. Humour is about people, about how they react to all those things the travel guides describe, as well as how they react to each other. Humour couldn't care less about *what* will serve us best; it prefers to look at *who* will manage not to. It's interested not in where we set down our bags, but in the baggage we all carry with us: awe and delight, playfulness and absurdity, dreams and nightmares, myths and stereotypes, platitudes and pretensions, expectations and obsessions, anger and fear and love.

This is a book about travelling in *England,* among the *English,* not in Great Britain among the British. Humour is based largely on familiarity, and the rest of the world knows very little about the rest of the island; there is little about the Welsh that doesn't simply make fun of their language, and little about the Scots that doesn't refer to their being cheap. We've included two token British pieces: one on climbing Mt. Snowdon in Wales, the other on grouse-hunting in Scotland.

Yes, *In a Fog* is more than just another pretty guidebook. Behind its sparkling veneer is a serious humour anthology, a treasury of the best humorous writing about travelling in England, by humorists who travel and travel writers who have a sense of humour. Among the selections are many that are simply fun or silly or nonsensical, many that make unusual or ironic observations, many that satire or parody or find some other way to poke fun at, many that take delight in what they see, and some that do all of these at once. Although many of the selections are vintage, little of the humour here is about the way things used to be; it's too easy to laugh at our fathers and grandmothers. This is a book about the way things are and will, most likely, be.

In a Fog contains a good mix of the work of the famous, the once famous, and the relatively obscure. Most readers will recognize the names of Robert Benchley, Art Buchwald, Theodore Dreiser, Nathaniel Hawthorne, Henry James, Will Rogers, Paul Theroux, and Mark Twain. Less well known these days, but well loved often not long ago are such writers as George Ade, Emily Kimbrough, Eric Knight, Stephen Leacock, Phyllis McGinley, Ruth McKenney, Christopher Morley, Petroleum V. Nasby, H. Allen Smith, Frank Sullivan, and

*"I warned you that draughts are not the
same thing as air conditioning."*

Mahood

Artemus Ward. We have also included the viewpoints of foreign-language authors such as Israeli humorists Ephraim Kishon and Hanock Bartov, French humorist Pierre Daninos, Czechoslovak author Karel Capek, Spanish native George Santayana, and English non-humorists W. H. Hudson, H. V. Morton, and W. Somerset Maugham. And finally, one notable but unknown writer whose book on her travels in England deserves special mention: Margaret Halsey, author of *With Malice Toward Some*.

Well, that's enough names. Now you won't have to read the table of contents. Enjoy the book, by the glass, the pint, or the yard, however you like.

❧Preparations

❧*How can one prepare for England? Americans as well as Canadians prepare for it all their lives. When we're born, we're often compared, favorably and unfavorably, to the latest royal babe. We seem to learn the kings of England even before we learn our presidents. We constantly hear English accents on television, and from the way the adults react, we seem to think they're something special unless, of course, they're Cockney or the like. At school we read their three-volume novels and epic poems and plays, and at home we listen to their more contemporary music. Before we know it, we too are following their royalty's love lives. We too are starting to like Burberry raincoats and Laura Ashley dresses. At last, our aspiration is to make a pilgrimage and see where all the kings and queens, and lords and ladies, and vicars and their wives hung their hats, and crowns.*

Not long ago one of America's most popular humorists, H. Allen Smith was in just such a position before making his first trip to England. Let him tell you how he prepared to travel to the nation that adopted us and then brought us up to a young, revolutionary adulthood.

H. Allen Smith
Some Good Advice 1952

PHILOSOPHERS OF EVERY AGE have emphasized the essential quality of good manners, and even the great cynics among our wise men have told us that common civility and nicety of conduct are required of man if he is to expect anything approaching happiness on earth. It was an ancient Chinese sage who counseled: "Never pick your nose or your ear except with your elbow."

Strange that we Americans, who have achieved so much, have achieved so little. I have long been aware of the fact that we are rude, crude, brash, arrogant, blabber-mouthed and, in the eyes of other peoples, singularly repulsive. I stand prepared to confess myself as one of the worst of the lot. Within the intimacy of this, my journal, I am compelled to admit that I am an uncouth, boorish and bombastic man. I ain't suave.

The hour for improvement is long overdue. I have reached the time of life where I require dignity and a measure of self-respect to go with the graying hair at my temples. I am vulgar and raucous and smug—then I must do something to correct this condition. I want people to say, "He's nice."

All my life I have heard about that enviable creature, the English Gentleman. There is no crudity, no vulgarity, no *gaucherie,* in the English character. So it is said. I have heard that there is no Emily Post in England. They know, instinctively, the value of the soft voice, the courtly bow, the graceful curtsy, and making a leg. Among all the peoples of the world they are the most urbane and therefore the most admirable.

I have decided to go live amongst them for a while, to observe them in their homes and on their streets and in their offices. I shall stay with them for an indefinite period, until such time as I have cured myself of the faults in my personality. * * *

[Recently] I happened onto a book written by a certain Boswell. He, too, had gone to London to better himself, and his manner of life in the British capital seemed admirably suited to my own purposes. He drank a good deal and spent much of his time just talking to people and listening to people talk. He did a good many other things which I thought would be quite nice. His ambition was to get a commission in the Guards, provided they would furnish him with a guarantee that he would not be sent anywhere to fight. He yearned to be the kind of soldier who bangs away at nothing, but he was always being turned down and in his frustration he'd go out and bang away at anything that fell in his path.

I spoke to Mistress Nelle of my enthusiasm for this Boswell, pointing out that he was quite young at the time he wrote his journal, and that I would be an idiot to try to pattern my behavior after his. I replied that I wanted to get to know the people of London and that you can't get to know people without having intercourse with them. Something about the way I stated my case caused her to bristle, and she said she would have to insist upon one thing—I was not to be hanging around stage doors.

We went down to Rockefeller Center and had our passport pictures taken. There was a sign on the wall in the long, narrow studio, which said: PASSPORT PICTURES MUST NOT BE RE-TOUCHED. WRINKLES, LINES IN FACE (AND THROAT) MUST NOT BE REMOVED. POUCHES UNDER EYES, FRECKLES, BIRTHMARKS ETC. MUST NOT BE REMOVED. We removed nothing, but sat with our pouches and wrinkles until we were summoned. These people take the pictures as fast as a man can candle eggs and we were apprehensive about the results, knowing we would look grotesque, and then the prints were ready. Never before in our lives had either of us taken such flattering pictures; I reflected on the fact that nothing is ever quite as bad as it's painted, except politicians, hangovers, marriage and cancer.

Now all of our acquaintances who have either been to Europe or who have seen travelogues in the newsreels began plying us with advice. The kind of clothes to take. Best places to eat. How to cheat the customs. How to trade in black markets. Important people to look up. And what Nelle should buy in London. At this point I issued a big fat ukase. I said that we were taking four suitcases. There was to be no buying of anything. We were not going to England to shop. We were not going to load ourselves down with junk. If we wanted to shop we could shop in White Plains. The womenfolk were horrified at my position. They said it was unthinkable that anyone would go to Europe without buying a few things. Clothes. Perfume. Silverware. Antique furniture. Bicycles. Small automobiles. Shards from the Wren churches shattered in the blitz. But I stood firm, and got so wrought up about the matter that I announced that Nelle could not go unless she promised she would buy nothing. She promised.

We were warned that we should take an assortment of medicines, including plenty of miracle drugs, and bandages, and soap in bars and in flakes and, above all, toilet paper. Almost everyone urged us to carry our own toilet paper. I sat down and started calculating and then consulted with my traveling companion and finally arrived at the conclusion that we would need to take toilet tissue equivalent to the weight of our four suitcases and ourselves, plus one roll for a friend. At this point I almost abandoned the entire project, but we settled the matter by deciding to put our trust in the finer sensitivity of the English people.

What's especially nice about going to England is that you don't have to buy a phrasebook and either brush up on or try to learn a foreign language. We don't have to worry if a restaurant or a passerby speaks our language. Everyone is fair game in England.

Or are they? Sure, they speak English, but as far as they're concerned, we speak American or Canadian. So, since traditional guidebooks don't have the nerve to include a short glossary of useful phrases, we've lined up Professor Charles E. Frank and Mses. Frances Douglas and Thelma Lecocq to give us, respectively, an introductory and intermediate course in the Queen's English (officially known as "received pronunciation," as if it were handed down from someone higher than the Queen Herself). And then we have for you an actual glossary, compiled by none other than H. Allen Smith.

Charles E. Frank
Isn't Tit? 1967

DON'T REMEMBER NOW WHERE IN LONDON I saw the sign, but I do remember how it read:

> Ici On Parle Francais
> Deutsch Gesprochen
> English Spoken
> American Understood

It may have been intended as whimsy, or it may have voiced a rebuke, but whatever the intention there is truth in it. An American expects to have some language difficulties in France or Italy, but he finds it more than frustrating when an Englishman stares at him as blankly as an Italian.

The causes are obvious enough: for many common things we have different words altogether. Take motoring, for example. Gasoline is petrol, a truck is a lorry, a traffic circle is a roundabout. Reversing the order, the bonnet is the hood, the boot is the trunk, and a lay-by is a place to draw off the road and have a look at a map, take in the view, or brew a cup of tea.

When it isn't vocabulary, it's idiom. One evening shortly after we had arrived in London we walked by an excavation and observed the wooden wall that kept pedestrians from falling in. Neatly labeling it in block letters was the inscription:

BILL STICKERS WILL BE PROSECUTED

Connie's puzzled question, "What has Bill done?" started the twins on a series of wild speculations, and they were disappointed when I explained that this legend was the equivalent of our

POST NO BILLS

Some English expressions at first sound quaint, but soon they seem peculiarly appropriate, and you wonder why you ever thought them odd. We lived near the Hammersmith Flyover, which we found a delightful piece of architecture as well as an absurd piece of traffic engineering. It is a couple of miles of elevated highway intended to carry heavy traffic over a congested area. Although cars did seem to fly for that short distance, at rush hours there was only a sluggish movement at either end, so the term "flyover" was used with irony by pedestrians and with contempt by motorists.

Another expression that fascinated us was the warning: "Mind the zebra!" We knew that the English loved all creeping, crawling things, and that their city traffic was stalled by all sorts of obstructions—but a zebra! Well, a zebra is a pedestrian crossing, with wide black and white lines painted across the street and flashing yellow globes at either end. Knocking down pedestrians on a zebra is not cricket, though some drivers, especially those in perky little minicars, make every zebra crossing something of an adventure, both for themselves and for pedestrians.

Food can be tricky. For breakfast you may be offered bubble-and-squeak (a kind of fried cabbage-and-potato hash, with a little bit of meat mixed in). A roast is a joint, hamburger is mince (or, commercially, a Wimpy), cookies are biscuits, French fries are chips, and potato chips are potato crisps. "Elevenses" describes that hiatus we call a coffee break, and tea is likely to be a fairly substantial meal, unless it is referred to as a "cuppa." Cider is a favorite drink, but if it is Somerset draught cider you'd better go easy, because that kind packs the wallop of a very dry martini.

Clothing can also be confusing. Knickers are women's underpants, pants are men's underpants and never a synonym for trousers, vests are undershirts, and waistcoats are vests. Nappies are diapers, Plimsolls are sneakers, Wellingtons are boots, a mac is a raincoat, and a cheater is a windproof jacket. Braces are suspenders, suspenders are garters, and a brolly, thank God, is an umbrella.

When you've got the vocabulary and a smidgen of idiom, you can then pay attention to pronunciation. Most of us are familiar with the British alu*min*ium, cen*teen*ary, and la*bor*at'ry from having heard Winston Churchill or Laurence Olivier or David Frost say them. But con*trover*sy, schedule pronounced with a "sh" and margarine with a hard "g" require a little time to get used to. Of course, proper names have their own laws: Cockburn is *Coburn,* St. John is *Sinjin,* and Beaulieu is *Bewley.* There must be a bookful of jokes about the situations all this can lead to. Like the one about the English lady named Margot who got irritated when Jean Harlow kept calling her by her first name, and mispronouncing it at that. Finally she could take it no longer: "The 't' is silent, dear, as in Harlow." Or the one about the American who got tired of having his pronunciation of such names as Cholmondeley and Leicester corrected. He began to refer to his home town of Niffles. His host finally bit, and said he didn't think he'd ever heard of that place. Said the American: "No doubt you've been mispronouncing it Niagara Falls."

When you think you've mastered the pronunciation, you have still got to cope with the intonation, which is very nearly indescribable. There is something about the rise and fall of the Englishman's pitch that strikes most Americans as downright fruity. On the other hand, the even tenor of the American pitch is likely to make the Englishman think he's conversing with a monotone. A Quaker friend told me a story that illustrates the difference between American and English intonation. After spending several years in England he had returned to his upstate New York home. Shortly after his return, a young woman he had known all his life telephoned to welcome him back. They talked for a while, and his mother overheard part of the conversation. When he had hung up she said, "Arnold, what's come over thee? Why should a nice girl want to talk to thee when thee answers her as if she were dirt under thy feet?" There it is in a nutshell. American speech is likely to be easy-going and relaxed to the point of sloppiness. English speech is likely to be clipped and precise to the point of snobbery. The Englishman no more thinks he is a snob than the American thinks he is a slob, but this is the effect the one often has on the other.

Of course, there is no such thing as an English accent, for they don't all talk in the same way any more than we do. What we mean when we speak of an English accent is usually either that of early Eliza Doolittle in *My Fair Lady,* or the so-called Oxford accent, used by BBC announcers and Archbishops of Canterbury. Between these extremes there are countless variations that only a Professor Higgins could distinguish. I can tell a Kentishman from a Lancashire lass, or an Irishman from a Welshman, but the difference between the accents of Durham and Yorkshire eludes me. Liverpool and Birmingham, though not far apart, are said to have dialects as distinct as those of Brooklyn and Baltimore, but I cannot vouch for this.

In addition to geography, class makes a difference in both vocabulary and intonation. The awful word "bloody" seems to be offensive chiefly to the lower middle class. An alternative, acceptable in some quarters, is "flippin'"—don't ask me why.

The female bus conductor will lean over you maternally and say, "What'll it be, luv?" And when you've paid up, you are likely to get a cheery, "Ta, dearie." Your wife will get the same sort of tender language from the greengrocer, who will none the less quietly set straight her pronunciation: When she orders a pound of "to*may*toes," he will respond, "A pound of to*mah*toes, yes, luv."

I suppose the speech quirk that bugged me most was the national habit of tacking a leading question onto a muddled statement, enunciating the question with agonizing clarity: "We wouldn't want to mumble mumble jumble, *would we now?*" Once, inadvertently, I learned how to deal with this maneuver. Someone said to me, "It's a very fortunate thing that hocus-pocus, hanky-panky, willy-nilly, *isn't tit?*" Irritated, I said emphatically, *"Tit isn't!"*

Whereupon we both laughed and went on to something less laden with con*tro*versy.

Frances Douglas & Thelma Lecocq
The English Language
**HOW IT CAME TO BE THE STRANGE
THING IT IS TODAY** 1946

ENGLAND IS A COUNTRY of many dialects. Half the people don't know what the other half are saying half the time, and wouldn't be on speaking terms with them if they did.

This is a deplorable state of affairs that zoologists, ornithologists, and the S.P.C.A. have tried for generations to explain. The result is a number of conflicting theories that don't get anybody anywhere, but only bring forth a lot of new words, mostly Greek and Latin, that none of the people understand.

The favourite is the theory that the English aren't English at all. Instead of that they're Romans, Celts, Saxons, Danes, Frenchmen, and Americans, and it follows quite naturally that they couldn't possibly understand each other. This theory, however, is not considered a very good one, as you can't find an Englishman anywhere who'll admit to being anything but an Englishman.

The latest theory (our own, patent pending) is generally known as *Writer's Cramp*. This means simply that the English are cramped by having so many writers in their country and instead of being Romans, Danes, et cetera, who can't understand each other they become Hardyians, Phillpottians, Walpolians, Laurentians, Webbians, and so forth, who still don't understand each other.

The secret of this dates back to the days when a blighter named Caxton invented the printing jenny and the English were so proud of him that Parliament passed the Thirty-Nine Articles whereby everyone was compelled to read all the books that were published (then numbering thirty-nine, of course).

This was all very fine until there began to be more books and the poor oppressed people began to groan under the weight of them. After a time they rebelled and we have the famous Industrial Revolution when they burned the printing jenny as a witch, and the Inquisition when books were burned and also the clergy (it being suspected that many of them had written three-volume novels). After that somebody thought of democracy and the people were allowed to vote on what books they'd read. Devon, for example, returned Mr. Phillpotts at the polls; Dorset, Mr. Hardy, and so on.

Then, in order to show that they'd read these books, people began to talk like Mr. Phillpotts and Mr. Hardy and the others. This is the origin of the modern habit of quoting without quotation marks.

Thus, unless the tourist is very well read, conversation will be difficult for him. He has to remember that the Dorset 'furz' is a vegetable and not an animal as you'd suppose—while in the Wodehouse country an 'old muffin' is the *Homo sapiens* and not a stale tea bun, no matter what the dictionary says.

This takes us back to the theory that the countryside is best done from Havana or Juan Les Pins. However, if you must actually visit it, equip yourself with complete sets of Hardy, Phillpotts, Walpole, D. H. Lawrence (omit Lady Chatterley, nobody you'll meet will talk like that), Jeffery Farnol, Mary Webb, and any others you can think of. You won't need more than two hundred volumes altogether.

If, however, you take our advice and do the country-side via H. V. Morton or à la Charrybanc, you can devote your time to the more cosmopolitan speech of London. Here, two writers will give you all the background you need and you can go anywhere provided you've read Mr. Aldous Huxley (Chelsea) and Mr. P. G. Wodehouse (Mayfair). If you can't get them straight, stick to Wodehouse, who while Chelsea-ites will wrinkle up their noses if you call them 'chump' or 'chappie,' Mayfair-ites positively will throw you out if you refer to your navel or call your host a bloody swine.

Therefore we advise that you do London à la Wodehouse. You begin by *'buzzing about the metrop'*— then, if you are able to keep up with butlers, morning coats, Ascot ties, and silk hats, you may be *'slated for a lunch'* (i.e. invited to *'insult the old tum'*)—be asked to *'buzz up'* (you have to be on very intimate terms for this one)—or perhaps receive an invitation to *'swing a dashed efficient toe.'*

If you have a 'fair amount of the stuff' (i.e. *money*)—or have a *flesh-and-blood* (i.e. relative) in Burke's *Peerage*, you will be accepted (not enthusiastically, of course— that wouldn't do at all—but insultingly—which is a great compliment). You will know you've arrived when you hear yourself addressed as:

chappie	*egg*
blighter	*old crumpet*
chump	*fat-headed worm,* or
greedy hog	*wretched, pie-faced wambler.*

At this point it is wise to adapt yourself. You must cease to *remark* and begin to *gargle*. A *fine day* will become a *juicy morning*. An *idea* will be a *ripe suggestion*. *Taking a drink* becomes *mixing a spot*. You must take to wearing *whangers*—learn to *brace up and bite the bullet*—to *jerk up the total*—to *breeze off* to anywhere you had thought of going. And remember! All nouns must be prefixed by *dashed, hanged, mouldy, grim,* or *putrid*.

Having achieved this, you have reached the peak in your study of the language, and so we'll leave you. (By now you wouldn't be speaking to people like us, anyway.)

H. Allen Smith
Glossary 1952

English	American
Advert	Ad
Arf	Half
Bad show. . . .	Unfavorable state of affairs
Bash	Belt
Bed-sit	Two-room soot
Blost	God damn
Bloody	Durned
Bostard . . .	Stinker
Chuhs	Cheers
Conwenience . .	Rest room
Crikey	Judas Priest
Culchuh . . .	Culcher
Ebb-so-lutely . .	Absuhlootly
Eck-tually . . .	Akchelly
Extrordnry . . .	Extraordinairy
Flicks	Movies
Flicker off . . .	Get lost
Good show . . .	Favorable state of affairs
Groundnuts . .	Peanuts
Hols	Vacation
Hyah	Hear
Kyuh	Thank you
Labourite . . .	Democrat
Muckin . . .	Messin
Nat-your-a-lee . .	Natcherly
Nonsense . . .	Female bosom
One	You
Oss	Beast of burden
Paps	Perhaps

English					American
Plaz	.	.	.	.	Player's
Respectable	.	.	.	Dull
Shed-jewel	.	.	.	.	Skedgle
Sin	.	.	.	.	Saint
Titfer	.	.	.	.	Hat
Tory	.	.	.	.	Republican
Turning	.	.	.	Street corner
Up	.	.	.	.	Down
Yuhs	.	.	.	.	Years
Zed	.	.	.	.	Z

❧*Customs is always something to look forward to. No matter how much you plan for it, no matter how much you worry about it, no matter how successful you are at putting it out of your mind, it'll manage to surprise you. Here to give you two possible approaches to what awaits you when you get off the boat or plane, are Canada's great classic humorist Stephen Leacock, and Margaret Halsey, a woman whose book on England sums it up perhaps better than anyone else's. Then, to round out this chapter, novelist Theodore Dreiser describes his first night in England.*

Stephen Leacock
Extraordinary Behavior 1922

I PASS OVER ALSO THE INCIDENTS of my landing at Liverpool, except perhaps to comment upon the extraordinary behavior of the English Customs officials. Without wishing in any way to disturb international relations, one cannot help noticing the brutal and inquisitorial methods of the English Customs men as compared with the gentle and affectionate ways of the American officials at New York. The two trunks which I brought with me were dragged brutally into an open shed; the strap of one of them was rudely unbuckled, while the lid of the other was actually lifted at least four inches. The trunks were then roughly scrawled with chalk, the lids slammed-to, and that was all. Not one of the officials seemed to care to look at my things or to have the politeness to pretend to want to. I had arranged my dress suit and my pyjamas so as to make as effective a display as possible: a New York Customs officer would have been delighted with it. Here they simply passed it over. "Do open this trunk," I asked one of the officials, "and see my pyjamas." "I don't think it is necessary, sir," the man answered. There was a coldness about it that cut me to the quick.

But bad as is the conduct of the English Customs men, the immigration officials are even worse. I could not help being struck by the dreadful carelessness with which people are admitted into England. There are, it is true, a group of officials said to be in charge of immigration, but they know nothing of the discriminating care exercised on the other side of the Atlantic.

"Do you want to know," I asked of one of them, "whether I am a polygamist?"

"No, sir," he said very quietly.

"Would you like me to tell you whether I am fundamentally opposed to any and every system of government?"

The man seemed mystified. "No, sir," he said, "I don't know that I would."

"Don't you care?" I asked.

"Well, not particularly, sir," he answered.

I was determined to arouse him from his lethargy.

"Let me tell you, then," I said, "that I am an anarchistic polygamist, that I am opposed to all forms of government, that I object to any kind of revealed religion, that I regard the State and property and marriage as the mere tyranny of the bourgeoisie, and that I want to see class

19

hatred carried to the point where it forces every one into brotherly love. Now, do I get in?"

The official looked puzzled for a minute. "You are not Irish, are you, sir?" he said.

"No."

"Then I think you can come in all right," he answered.

Margaret Halsey
Filling in the Blanks 1938

WHILE HENRY HAS GONE to buy chocolate bars and reading matter, I am sitting in the waiting room of the Southampton station of the Southern Railway. My eyes, I am afraid, are going to fall right out of their sockets before the end of the day—I have been looking at everything so strenuously. It took a long while to get off the boat, and involved a great deal of standing in line and filling out cards and blanks. There is something about filling out printed forms which arouses lawless impulses in me and makes me want to do things that will have the file clerks sitting up with a jerk, like putting in

RELIGION.........*Druid*

Today, when one of my blanks said OCCUPATION, I wrote down *none,* though I suspected this would not do. A severe but courteous official confirmed this impression. So I crossed it out and wrote *parasite*, which, not to be too delicate about it, is what I am. This made the official relax a little and he himself put *housewife* in what space there was left. "Be a prince," I said. "Make it *typhoid carrier.*" But he only smiled and blotted out *parasite* so that it would not show.

Theodore Dreiser
First Night 1912

IT IS CURIOUS—THIS FEELING of being quite alone for the first time in a strange land. I began to unpack my bags, solemnly thinking of New York. Presently I went to the window and looked out. One or two small lights burned afar off. I undressed and got into bed, feeling anything but sleepy. I lay and watched the fire flickering on the hearth. So this was really England, and here I was at last—a fact absolutely of no significance to any one else in the world, but very important to me. An old, old dream come true! And it had passed so oddly—the trip— so almost unconsciously, as it were. We make a great fuss, I thought, about the past and the future, but the actual moment is so often without meaning. Finally, after hearing a rooster crow and thinking of Hamlet's father— his ghost—and the chill that invests the thought of cock-crow in that tragedy, I slept.

Karel Capek

London

Rarely do tourists go to England without going to London, and many tourists go nowhere else. London is where the stores are, the museums, the theater, the Thames, Big Ben and Little Dorrit. For the businessman, it's home to the City. For the diplomat, it's the capital. For the researcher, there's the British Museum. And for the tourist, there's ... well, let's leave all that for the sightseeing section.

London is, like most people we love, more than the sum of its parts. No matter what they do to it, no matter how crowded it gets, whether the party in power is Labour or Tory, it's always London. It may not be the center of an empire anymore; it may not be the center of Allied resistance; it may even, some day, stop setting trends in fashion and music. But these are only incidentals. London isn't fazed. For London is English, after all.

First off, the splendid American storyteller Christopher Morley will tell us how one of his characters felt on his first visit to London. Then another of America's most delightful storytellers, Ruth McKenney (with her husband, Richard Bransten), and Israeli travel writer Hanock Bartov will advise us how to get around London, and how much the difficulties in getting around tell us about the place and its people.

Christopher Morley
A Perspective Experience 1926

WHAT HE REMEMBERED BEST of those first days in London was an extraordinary sense of freedom; freedom not merely from external control but also from the uneasy caperings of self. To be in so great a city, unknown and unregarded, was to have the privileged detachment of a god. It was a cleansing and perspective experience, one which few of our gregarious race properly relish. He had no business to transact, no errand to accomplish, no duty to perform. Only to enjoy, to observe, to live in the devotion of the eye. So, in his quiet way, he entered unsuspected into circulation, passing like a well-counterfeited coin. Comedy herself, goddess of that manly island, seemed unaware of him. Occasionally, in the movement of the day, he saw near him others who were evident compatriots, but he felt no impulse to hail and fraternize. The reticence of that vastly incurious city was an excellent sedative. Once he got out his *My Trip Abroad* album to record some impressions, but desisted after a few lines. "I felt too modest to keep a diary," was his explanation.

Except for the left-hand traffic, which cost him some rapid skipping on street crossings, he encountered no phenomena of surprise. London seemed natural, was exactly what it should be. At first the dusky light led him to believe, every morning, that some fierce downpour was impending; but day after day moved through gossamer tissues and gradations of twilight, even glimmered into cool fawn-coloured sunshine, without the apparently threatened storm. In the arboured Bloomsbury squares morning lay mild as yellow wine; smoke of burning leaves sifted into the sweet opaque air. Noon softly thickened into evening; evening kept tryst with night.

His conviction of being in fairyland, when I come to put down what he said, seemed to rest on very trifling matters. The little hotel where he stayed was round the corner from a post office, and in an alley thereby were big scarlet vans, with horses, and initialled by the King. These ruddy wagons in the dusk, the reliable shape of policemen's helmets and boots, a bishop in the hotel who fell upon his breakfast haddock as though it were a succulent heresy, the grossness of "small" change, and a black-gowned bar lady in a *bodega* who served glasses of sherry with the air of a duchess—these were some of the details he mentioned. His description of men in the subway, sitting in seats with upholstered arms, smoking pipes and wearing silk hats, was, perhaps, to a New Yorker, more convincing suggestion of sorcery. But apparently the essence of London's gramarye was just that there were no shocking surprises. Fairyland should indeed be where all the incongruous fragments of life might fall into place, and things happen beautifully without indignation or the wrench of comedy. London seemed so reasonable, natural, humane, and polite. If ever you felt any inclination to be lonely or afraid, he said, the mere look of the taxicabs was reassuring. They were so tall and bulky and respectable; they didn't look "fast," their drivers were settled and genteel. He even formed an idea that London fairies, if encountered, would wear very tiny frock coats and feed on the daintiest minuscule sausages; with mustard, of course; and miniature fried fish after the theatre.

Ruth McKenney & Richard Bransten
Getting Around 1950

FOR AN AMERICAN, the quality of London is subtle, and in the beginning, difficult.

This, I may as well admit, is a high-toned way of saying that the first time I saw London, I was shocked by anti-climax. But now, like most converts, I am didactic. I think London is the most beautiful and the most fascinating city in the world. Bar none.

"Oh, *really?*" Richard says, looking bland.

I must explain that my husband has loved London since his careless youth, June, 1927. The day we arrived at Victoria Station (August, 1948), Richard was aflame to show his wife the city he had remembered so fondly across twenty-one years. So, as we chugged along in our matronly, high-slung taxi, he announced, in a voice charged with emotion, "Look, darling! London! the greatest city in the world!"

"Where?" I cried, hanging feverishly out the taxi window.

"Where! What-do-you-mean-where?"

I should have caught a certain coldness in my husband's tones, but I was too excited to take proper notice of domestic nuance. I thought we had arrived at some dingy suburban station, and were even now driving through the flat, unappetizing fringes of the English metropolis. "How far is it? To the main part, I mean?"

"This," Richard replied between his teeth, "is Piccadilly Circus."

I gaped. I was certainly taken aback. Piccadilly Circus has all the charm of Columbus Circle, New York City, and not half the pomp of Public Square in Cleveland, Ohio. There is a small statue of Eros and a large but inferior beer sign.

"Oxford Street," Richard said presently.

"Oh?"

Richard became exasperated. "What do you want, the Empire State Building? Or the Arc de Triomphe? Listen, this is the most sophisticated, civilized city in history; don't be so damned *provincial.*"

Provincial is not a word which, in my opinion, can be bandied about lightly. We arrived at our hotel, after my first taxicab tour of the capital of the British Commonwealth, in an icy mood. Furthermore, the plumbing proved to be aggressively quaint, and we had raspberry trifle for dinner. The trifle reduced even Richard to a state of melancholy; he began to talk about the Decline of the Empire Builders. Indeed, as we started out for a stroll in the August twilight, Richard was working on an interesting theory that raspberry trifle probably began with the Boer War as a kind of national self-mortification. "Imagine Shakespeare, Sir Walter Raleigh, or Cromwell eating trifle! I'm afraid this whole trifle-kipper-limp-cabbage school of eating marks the decay of a once proud people. I wonder if Ruskin invented trifle?"

"Maybe Walter Pater?"

"Or take this thing they call toad-in-the-hole. Whimsy is a very dangerous thing for the moral fiber of a nation. If you ask me, Peter Pan was the beginning of the end...."

* * *

Everything about London is difficult, in the beginning. It appears to have no logic, no solid center, no starting point. In Paris, you soon learn to know where you are in relation to the Champs-Elysées, the Louvre, the Boul' Mich'. The middle of Chicago is, obviously, the Loop. The Grand' Place is the heart of Brussels; and in Cleveland you start with Public Square, after which things are East or West, North or South.

But London—! Well, London is a series of medieval towns strung together along both sides of the Thames. The river, when you peer at it from bridges and embankments, *seems* reasonably straight. It isn't. The Thames makes two terrific bends, dislocating all the geography for miles. Westminster Abbey and the Royal Hospital, Chelsea, are both on the left-hand bank of the Thames; but a straight line drawn from the Abbey would end you up in Clapham Common, after which you must hire native beaters and unlatch your compass to get back to Trafalgar Square. The glorious dome of St. Paul's is visible from great distances; but it is hardly what I would call a landmark. From Victoria Embankment, the dome appears to be nobly shining *across* the Thames; a few blocks farther along, it has shifted and now glitters straight ahead, definitely on the *left-hand* river bank. This is very dubious behavior for a landmark. I say nothing of the fact that London streets change names as they go along, so that what is *The* Strand (definite article) suddenly turns into Fleet *Street,* to the consternation of the excitable bus traveler, who starts ringing bells and nervously throwing himself off platforms under the delusion that he has somehow started going in the wrong direction when he wasn't looking.

Londoners, who apparently acquire the geography of their city as a sixth sense, the way Americans learn batting averages, are fond of identifying Piccadilly Circus as the "heart" of the metropolis. I think this is an unprofitable, if not dangerous, concept for the visitor, who soon discovers that the Bank of England is a long, long way from Eros, and busses should be tackled from Charing Cross, not Piccadilly. Indeed, I lived in London for months before I was quite, quite sure how to get from Trafalgar to Leicester Square. If you look at the map, this project seems laughably easy—just a quick jog, down two side streets. In real life, Leicester Square is extremely slippery. I finally got it pinned down. After you get off the bus at Charing Cross, you turn back, and walk past the beautiful church of St. Martin-in-the-Fields. Some architects think the lantern spire is wrong, humpbacked, or awkward, but (for me, at least) it is lovely, especially on a foggy Sunday afternoon in winter. Besides, St. Martin's is queer, for an American; it is obviously the handsome stone model for half the little white wooden churches in New England. I remember an old church in Litchfield, Connecticut—set on the brow of a dark-green hill, surrounded by silence; a small white wooden church, with a clapboard spire, as exact a copy as the settlers could make with their saws and home-forged nails. I expect it is excessively sentimental, but the first time I saw St. Martin's in Trafalgar Square, my heart ached, abruptly, with a lurch, for the men who built the white wooden church in Litchfield so long ago. For I never realized before how homesick they must have been; how, all alone in the forbidding forests, they must have yearned after the dear places they would never see again. The church in Litchfield is wholly different from St. Martin's— it is innocent, simple, quite rude; St. Martin's is exquisitely sophisticated. But when you see the grace and mannered elegance of the spire you will remember the lonely white wooden steeple in Litchfield, Connecticut.

Trafalgar Square, I remarked. Charing Cross is just next to Trafalgar Square—an important point. St. Martin-in-the-Fields is across the street from the National Gallery. The National Gallery has one of the greatest collections of paintings under any roof in the world; there are so many splendid art collections in London that the natives are rather calm and blasé on the subject. "Oh, yes, the National Gallery," they say, "fine collection." So you wander in some Sunday afternoon and discover Michelangelos and Da Vincis and Van Dycks and Titians to make the mind reel. However, let us not get bemused. We are now progressing from Charing Cross (that is, Trafalgar Square, you see) to Leicester Square.

We've crossed the street to the National Gallery; now we turn our backs on the fountains and, with Nelson in the rear, march smartly forward, for a very short block.

Now comes a very tricky bit. One must be on the alert here or everything will go stupendously wrong, and the next thing one will be in Covent Garden.

I suppose everybody works out his own private street guide to London. I get from Charing Cross to Leicester Square by sighting on the man who ties himself up in a canvas sack and permits (indeed urges) bystanders to strangle him with a steel chain. This hideous drama is played by two men in appallingly dirty underwear. They operate just in back of the National Portrait Gallery, a little to the left of Sir Henry Irving's statue. The first man, evidently the manager, runs around bawling, hoarsely: "Strangle 'im! Come on, strangle 'im!" Meantime, the hero has taken off his shirt, revealing, as I remarked, under-wear of a nature to make the fastidious turn pale; he wriggles into a stout, filthy canvas sack. The manager ties up the sack—a rope at the ankles, and one at the neck. Sightless, helpless, hideous, the sack now hops around horribly, providing the stuff that nightmares are made of.

At this spot, turn left, *past* the sack, and go down a little side street—and there is Leicester Square. Simple.

Hanock Bartov
A Harmony of Its Own 1969

ONE SHOULD NEVER DARE step out of the hotel without first writing down the precise name of the street and part of the city one wants to get to, and one must always include the tricky little cipher meant to indicate that W.12 is nowhere near W.1. Yet even after one has taken every possible precaution, the wayfarer's prayer is still in order. Do not expect to find a number on each house; a large building or court is quite likely to make do with no more than a mere Christian name. The logic is peculiar, but very English: it stands to reason that if you are someone who ought to know, you will; if you don't, proof enough you shouldn't, so please don't be a nuisance. * * *

As I kept losing my way and blundering about in its endless maze, the city somehow began to emerge for me; the beauty of London tucked away behind the disarray of houses glued together, winding in and out along its winding streets, sprawled out in its eternal drizzle, began to make a kind of sense. The total lack of a well-ordered system or logic which is London forms a harmony of its own, complex and fascinating. So numerous are its impressive edifices that a long, long time must pass before one can thrill to the discovery of a particular facade, a familiar curve of the Thames, a certain pub. Only then can one begin to conceive the sum-total of what millions have constructed here in the course of many generations, from the labyrinthine docks in the east to the City, commercial pulse of London; the political heart of the Empire, stretched out between St. Paul's and Westminster, Trafalgar Square, Buckingham Palace and Hyde Park. One gradually comes to recognise the styles of the different eras, in Knightsbridge, Regent's Park, Hampstead—an architectural Tower of Babel which makes it easier to understand the principles underlying Britain's social system. Just as Britain has no written Constitution, but an intricate network of Acts, Precedents, Usages and Traditions, so nothing works here in accordance with some preconceived and detailed master-plan forced upon it from an omniscient central authority. A master-plan of this kind was once devised following the Great Fire, but the English—stiff-necked and jealous guardians of their own eccentric egos—managed to outwit that as well. Yet again, with all the British objection to conformity, with everybody endeavouring to be out of step, as it were, the sum-total of all these eccentricities is more harmonious than any master-plan, and not one whit less English than the familiar stock-types of anecdotes and satire.

London is such a special, not to mention enormous place, that no one who goes there can truly sum it up. Each of us sees only a limb of its body, a nation of its planet, a galaxy of its universe. Do we really have the right to even comment on it? Isn't anything we could venture to say as false as saying that London is a wee village surrounded by rolling meadows leading up to vast mountain ranges on all sides? I think so. Therefore, to sum it up, to capture its very essence, we have turned to the one man capable of seeing London whole, the one man courageous enough to write about London without ever having left New York: Frank Sullivan, America's most heroic travel writer.

Frank Sullivan
A Visit to London
By One Who Has Never Been There 1939

WE ARRIVED IN LONDON IN A FOG. The great sprawling metropolis was completely enveloped in a pea-soup mist which, we were told, had descended a month and a half previously. We didn't mind, because somehow it seemed right that we should have our first sight of the great sprawling metropolis in a fog. Nell's only regret was that on account of the fog we could only get a dim view of the famous old Waterloo Station, which we heard had been built on the cricket fields of Eton.

Nell wanted to put up at one of the fashionable caravansaries in Tooting Bec, but I vetoed that. I told her as long as we were in London we ought to try to get the flavor of the great sprawling metropolis (which I shall refer to from now on as London) by stopping at one of those cosy old inns replete with historical interest and devoid of modern plumbing. Nell then suggested we go to the Cheshire Cheese, but I demurred again. I wanted to stop at the famous old inn frequented by Dr. Johnson and those other noted Regency bucks, but for the life of me I couldn't think of the name of the place, so to the Cheshire Cheese we went.

It proved utterly charming, exactly as we had pictured an old English inn—mullioned windows, mullioned waiters, ceilings with broad beams, barmaids with broader beams, et cetera. There was a room where Queen Elizabeth hid from Essex and his army, and another room where she hid with Essex and his army, and a third room where Essex and his army later hid from her.

There was a room where Shakespeare had been arrested for poaching and a room where Charles I hid from the Parliament while the Parliament was hiding from him in the room next door, which was the same room where Titus Oates hatched his plot. It was called the Plot Hatching Room on account of the fact that Guy Fawkes had also hatched his plot there.

Off the kitchen was a room where King Alfred let the cakes burn. And the tapster looked exactly like Sam Weller. Nell and I were delighted at our good fortune in finding such a really mellow old place.

We hired the Plot Hatching Room and proceeded to make ourselves comfortable. Both Nell and I had been looking forward with considerable interest to tasting British food, and we were not disappointed, for we dined excellently: a typical English meal of clotted Devonshire cream, roast beef, port wine and plum pudding. Afterward we took a tram (short for terambulator) to His Majesty's Theatre in Ludgate Circus and there saw a play by Noel Coward.

Next morning we were awakened bright and early by the cries of the hawksters, tipsters, drapers, mercers, et cetera, vending their wares in the streets below. (London newsboys are not permitted to shout their headlines.

They come up and whisper the news in your ear. This often tickles your ear, particularly if the whispered headline contains a lot of sibilants, such as "Lady Susan Sursingham Shoots Sire, Sir Seth Sursingham.")

There was a dense fog out. It was much denser than the pea-soup fog that had greeted our arrival. It was more the consistency of creamed cauliflower soup. You could scarcely see Windsor Castle.

A rosy-cheeked serving wench who reminded Nell of Sam Weller came in and laid a fire of sea coals and we breakfasted cosily by it. Typical English breakfast of clotted Devonshire cream, kedgeree, roast beef, Yorkshire pudding, mulled ale, crumpets, sack and port. The girl was curious about America and wanted to know if the Indians still used bows and arrows in attacking Manhattan. Then she asked if we would give her an Indian yell, so Nell and I obliged with the old Ojibway war cry:

"Cornell I yell yell yell Cornell!"

"Team Team Team!!!"

She was quite impressed, even a bit terrified.

We spent that day sightseeing and went in the evening to Their Majesties' Theatre to see a play. It was by Noel Coward.

What a fog next morning! I thought it was like *potage à la reine,* but Nell said it reminded her more of *borsch.* And those fascinating London noises, coming at you out of the mysterious fog. Nell and I are greatly interested in the noises characteristic of the various cities we visit. In Paris her favorite sound was the scrunch of the French burying the family sock, full of gold, in the backyard. Mine was the low hum of models posing for artists in the nude. Her favorite London noise was the click of pearl buttons dropping from costers' weskits, but I preferred the throaty drawl of duchesses snubbing persons in trade.

Nothing daunted by the fog, we sallied forth on our sightseeing, first taking the precaution of donning our raincoats, or waterproofs, as the English call them.

The English have the most peculiar words for things. Our subway, for instance, is their tube. I believe they have no word for our tube. They call baggage luggage; a cracker a lift, and an elevator a biscuit. Their meat is our poison and our drink is theirs. They call a spade a spade. In telephoning they say, "Are you there?" where we say, "Hello. Hello. Hello. Operator. Operator. Yes, they do answer. There's always somebody there. Ring them again."

The English are a great people for clipping their words, for making one syllable do the work of two or three. For instance, if an American were dining with a British lady of quality and he wanted the Worcestershire sauce, he would say, "Lady Ursula, could I trouble you for the Worcestershire sauce?" but an Englishman would say, "Lady Ursula, pass the Woosh."

On the other hand, they sometimes go to the other extreme. When they wish to express skepticism or incredulity they say, "Oh, I say now, not really, you know, what?" when we achieve the same effect by saying, "Nuts!" A London society woman says, "too perfectly divayne," where a New York society woman says, "too poifectly divine." And when the British want to express disapproval of conduct they consider unsportsmanlike or unethical they say, "That's not cricket," where we say, "That's probably wrestling."

One soon gets used to these little strangenesses. By the time we had been in London a week, nobody would have dreamed we were Americans had it not been for our tortoise-shell glasses, Nell's habit of chewing tobacco and saying, "Waal now, I reckon," and of course the large American flags she and I always carried.

The following day was Thursday and there was a really superb fog, like lobster bisque with toast Melba, I thought, but Nell said she saw it as cream of asparagus. She read in "The Old Lady of Threadneedle Street," as the British call the London *Times,* that a debate on the Boston

Tea Party was the order of the day in the House of Lords, so we gulped a typical English breakfast of fish and chips, jugged hare, and gin and bitters, and hurried over to the Houses of Parliament. But the debate was not very exciting and there was such a dense fog in the House of Lords that we couldn't see anything anyhow, so we went over to the Commons in the hope of hearing Lady Astor, the American-born peeress, in action.

They were debating the oakum situation in Woking (or it may have been the woking situation in Oakum) and the Prime Minister was being interrogated by the Opposition, Mr. Winston Churchill.

Next morning there was a glorious fog, just like oyster gumbo. I wanted to go over to Rotten Row to see the regatta, but Nell had her heart set on going down to Trafalgar Square to see the famous statue of Lord Nelson. This is the statue which according to the old story (see any high-school textbook in English history) tips its hat every time a virgin passes. We no sooner reached the Square than Lord Nelson tipped his hat to Nell. Not only tipped his hat to her but told her in a low but quite audible whisper that she reminded him of Sam Weller. Nell was furious, on both counts, and strode off muttering, "It's a fake. It's a fake."

Nell went shopping the next day but flopped badly. The shopkeepers wouldn't sell her anything because she had never been formally introduced to them. British shopkeepers are very strict about this. Nell came home angry and desperate.

"I need a new toothbrush," she wailed, "and I don't know a single druggist in London socially. What am I going to do?"

"Well, for one thing, don't say druggist," I warned her. In England a druggist is a chemist. A public school is a private school. The left side of the road is the right side, and gasoline is petrol. And "My Country 'tis of Thee" is "God Save the King."

That night we thought we'd go to Soho, the Italian or Bohemian quarter of London, as we had heard there were some very good Italian restaurants there. We found a very good one and dined magnificently for two and thruppence hapenny on clotted Devonshire cream, roast beef, bubble and squeak, ale and ravioli.

Passing through Upper Tooting on the way home, I was interested in seeing the offices of the famous humorous weekly *Punch*, or "The Thunderer," as the English affectionately call it. Once a week the staff of *Punch* lunch together and then, over the port, decide on the cover for the next week.

Nell and I liked the London cops, or bobbies, very much. They are a highly efficient body of men who wear chin straps and never allow a murderer to escape. Murder is rare in England and an unsolved murder is rarer. The low rate of homicide is due to the fact that the British never get well enough acquainted to kill each other. Once in a while a foreigner kills an Englishman for being too reticent, but if you see an Englishman murdering another Englishman you can be pretty sure the victim is either a blood relative or a friend of long standing.

The suicides in London are mainly foreigners driven to despair by attempts to understand the difference between the city with a small c and the City with a capital C. It seems that the City is part of the city, but the City is not all of the city. You can be in the city and not be in the City, but you cannot be in the City without being in the city. Nell spent two days trying to figure this out and then I had to take her to a nursing home, where she spent a week in a dense fog.

Our stay in London ended rather unexpectedly. After she returned from the nursing home Nell did not seem her usual self. Irritable and upset. One morning when I passed her the clotted Devonshire cream she glared at me and hissed, "I don't want any clotted Devonshire cream. See?"

And a moment later she added:

"Nor any clotted Yorkshire pudding either. See?"

I thought this rather odd. Nell generally has a good appetite and cleans her plate.

I looked out of the window after we finished breakfast.

"My, there's a magnificent fog out, Nell," I said, to make conversation. "Just like mulligatawny soup."

"It's not like mulligatawny soup at all," she snapped. "It's like clam chowder."

For some time past she had been growing more and more unreasonable on the subject of the fogs. It seemed to me she had an uncanny faculty for picking the wrong soup to fit a fog, and while much of the happiness of our life together has been based on mutual respect for each other's opinions, I considered this a plain question of fact on which it was my duty to set Nell right. The fog was certainly mulligatawny, not clam chowder. I told her so.

"The other day," I added, "when it really was clam chowder, you said it was like Philadelphia pepper pot."

She flew into a rage, told me that it was I who had been quoting the wrong soups all along; that she was sick of it, sick of the fogs and sick of me. With that she packed her bag and left for Cannes.

I dined alone at a pub that night and later went to a play. But somehow I could not enjoy it. Something was missing. Suddenly I realized what it was. The play was not by Noel Coward. I went home, restless and uneasy.

Another day went by and then, feeling very blue indeed, I was on the point of sending Nell a wire telling her she could name her own fogs if she would only come back, when a message arrived from her. It read as follows:

"Sorry I dusted off in such a huff. Lovely cream of tomato soup down here. Do come on down before it's all gone. Love, Nell."

I took the next train for Cannes.

London may always be London, but it is very different at different times of the year. That is part of being London, just as overbundling all winter and then donning a T shirt when the mercury hits 40 is part of being someone you know, or are. Here is novelist Henry James, an excellent travel writer in his youth, before he became a Londoner himself, on London in August; and classic American humorist George Ade on London at Christmastime.

Henry James
London in August c1875

BELIEVE IT IS SUPPOSED TO REQUIRE a good deal of courage to confess that one has spent the month of August in London; and I will therefore, taking the bull by the horns, plead guilty at the very outset to this dishonorable weakness. I might attempt some ingenious extenuation of it. I might say that my remaining in town had been the most unexpected necessity or the merest inadvertence; I might pretend I liked it—that I had done it, in fact, for the love of the thing; I might claim that you don't really know the charms of London until on one of the dog-days you have imprinted your boot-sole in the slumbering dust of Belgravia, or, gazing along the empty vista of the Drive, in Hyde Park, have beheld, for almost the first time in England, a landscape without figures. But little would remain of these specious apologies save the naked fact that I had distinctly failed to retire from the metropolis—either on the first of August with the ladies and children, or on the thirteenth with the members of Parliament, or on the twelfth when the grouse-shooting began. (I am not sure that I have got my dates right to a day, but these were about the proper opportunities.) I have, in fact, survived the departure of everything genteel, and the three millions of persons who remained behind with me have been witnesses of my shame.

I cannot pretend, on the other hand, that, having lingered in town, I have found it a very odious or painful experience. Being a stranger, I have not felt it necessary to incarcerate myself during the day and steal abroad only under cover of the darkness—a line of conduct imposed by public opinion, if I am to trust the social criticism of the weekly papers (which I am far from doing), upon the native residents who allow themselves to be overtaken by the unfashionable season. I have indeed always had a theory that few things are pleasanter than during the hot weather to have a great city, and a large house within it, quite to one's self.

These majestic conditions have not been combined in my own metropolitan sojourn, and I have received an impression that in London it would be rather difficult for a person not having the command of a good deal of powerful machinery to find them united. English summer weather is rarely hot enough to make it necessary to darken one's house and disrobe. The present year has indeed in this respect been "exceptional," as any year is, for that matter, that one spends anywhere. But the manners of the people are, to American eyes, a sufficient indication that at the best (or the worst) even the highest flights of the thermometer in the British Islands betray a broken wing. People live with closed windows in August, very much as they do in January, and there is to the eye no appreciable difference in the character of their apparel. A "bath" in England, for the most part all the year round, means a little portable tin tub and a sponge. Peaches and pears, grapes and melons, are not a more obvious ornament of the market at midsummer than at Christmas.

George Ade
Christmas in London 1922

WHEN YOU SET OUT TO QUALIFY as a circumnavigator, your whole timetable must be adjusted to seasonal conditions in India. Only in winter may the tourist in Agra, Jaipur, and Benares find protection under a pith helmet. Therefore, when two of us planned to go around the orange, following the most beaten track to the east, we began guessing at dates and destinations and learned that we would have to make an early start to avoid being trapped by the deadly heat so picturesquely advertised by Mr. Kipling.

All this copious prelude so that you may understand why we found ourselves in London at Christmas time. One needs an alibi in a case of that kind. Do you remember the melodrama, "Alone in London"? We appeared in it.

London on Christmas Eve was abuzz with gaiety (modified British gaiety) and crowds. We awoke on Christmas morning to find that during the night the human race had evaporated.

We got this first at the egg ceremony in the lonesome grill. It was repeated by the field marshal who stood at the main entrance. Also, this particular Christmas was spoken of very highly by the musical comedy hero who assigned the rooms.

Taking one 25th of December with another and striking an average, we would have said that this London Christmas was not even a dismal suggestion of the real thing.

A soft gloom covered the earth. The sky was a sombre canopy, compromising between a gray and a dun. If you should mix battleship color with the shade used in painting refrigerator cars, you might get an approximation of the effect. The light came from nowhere. Not freezing weather, but in the sluggish air a chill which cut right through top-coats.

But a jolly Christmas, nevertheless, because the fog had lifted and no rain was falling.

Probably we had been spoiled in the matter of Christmases. Our romantic specifications called for white draperies on the hillside, feathered plumes surmounting each thicket, the smoke from every chimney going straight up, and a steel-cold sun hanging in burnished splendor overhead.

We had made no plans for the day, somehow feeling that every Christmas works out its own program. Certainly we had looked forward to being in London on the day which English-speaking people have garlanded with so much of homely sentiment.

Probably we had a lot of Dickens still lurking in our systems. We rather hoped to find, in London at Yuletide, the carols ringing out on the frosty air, while the backlog roared, the punch-bowl was wreathed with spicy vapors, the boar's head smiled from its pillow of holly and, on every hand, crabbed old gentlemen melted perceptibly before the good cheer of the blessed day and began giving money to crippled children.

It may be that the English Christmas is just what has been represented to us in song and story, but the homeless transient sees no part of it.

As we walked forth that Christmas we found that the metropolis of the world had become merely an emptiness of walls and shutters. If machine-guns had been planted at Trafalgar Square to sweep each radiating thoroughfare, there would have been no fatalities.

Probably behind the high walls (spiked with broken glass) and the drawn shades, the nuts were being cracked and cobwebby bottles of old port were being tenderly operated upon, and Uncle Charleys with shining faces were proposing toasts.

But even a prohibition agent, intent upon compelling merrymakers to find their wassail in grape juice, would have been deceived by the outward solemnity of Christmas in London.

It seems to be the one day in the calendar on which every Englishman retires into his own home and pulls up the drawbridge. Those who have country places go to the country and those who know people having country places put in acceptances weeks ahead. At every hearthstone the relatives who have been shunned during the previous 364 days are stuffed with warm food.

So we were told.

By noon we decided to escape from our hotel. It was so near the Thames that we dared not trust ourselves.

We learned of an old tavern, miles up the river, where a special dinner was served on Christmas Day. Sure enough, we found a bed of coals in a grate, a Pickwick sort of person sitting in front of it, and a head waiter with apologetic side-whiskers.

We made out, as you might say, but if you, reader, are planning to be in Merrie England on Christmas Day, look up the forkings of the ancestral tree and try to discover a relative.

"City" Pub

Osbert Lancaster

❧ London Amusements

❧*Any time of year, there's an incredible amount to do and see in London. There's the best theater in the English-speaking world, but there's not much funny about that, unless—one hopes—it's a comedy. There's all that shopping to do on Oxford Street, Regent Street, and Brompton Road. There are all those familiar buildings to see, if for no other reason than to see if they're really how you imagined them: the Houses of Parliament, Westminster Abbey, St. Paul's, the Tower of London, and, not too far out of town, Hampton Court and Windsor Castle. Then the museums, one of which, the British Museum, could fill a week itself and still not give up a fraction of its mysteries; the parks, with their fountains and walks; and the sporting events, from tennis at Wimbledon to the races at Ascot, if your timing and connections are good. There are, to be sure, restaurants, roast beef and Yorkshire pudding, the whole shtick, but once you've got that under your belt, you might want to try the cuisines of those countries Britain has, at one time or another, colonized or simply defeated. And, of course, the many wondrous types of beer (if such a prosaic word can be applied, even in the most general sense, to poetic ales, bitters, and stouts). Finally, there are all those places—pubs, shops, Inns of Court—where your favorite writers and characters spent their days and nights. And each of them has books to guide you to and through them. Literary London. London's Museums. London Architecture. Shopping in London. Londoning London.*

Well, we realize that in these pages we can only touch on a small number of the major sights to see and things to do. We make no representations and accept no blame. We'd just as soon let you walk the streets without a single guide; you still couldn't help but see a lot of wonderful and awful sights, only different ones. So here's just a few looks at sightseeing in London. First, Mark Twain will look at St. Paul's—and art in general—from a point of view only he could ever manage to find. Then we'll visit the dreaded Tower of London with one of nineteenth-century America's greatest and most popular humorists, Artemus Ward; the labyrinth at Hampton Court with humorous American travel writer Willard Price; the British Museum with the indefatigable Mark Twain; and last, but not least, the part of London no one ever visits, guided by the great English travel writer H. V. Morton, since no furreners were available.

Mark Twain
Old Saint Paul's 1872

WHO CAN LOOK upon this venerable edifice, with its clustering memories and old traditions, without emotion! Who can contemplate its scarred and blackened walls without drifting insensibly into dreams of the historic past! Who can hold to be trivial even the least detail or appurtenance of this stately national altar! It is with diffidence that I approach the work of description, it is with humility that I offer the thoughts that crowd upon me.

Upon arriving at Saint Paul's, the first thing that bursts upon the beholder is the back yard. This fine work of art is forty-three feet long by thirty-four and a half feet wide—and all enclosed with real iron railings. The pavement is of fine oolite, or skylight, or some other stone of that geologic period, and is laid almost flat on the ground, in places. The stones are exactly square, and it is thought that they were made so by design; though of course, as in all matters of antiquarian science there are wide differences of opinion about this. The architect of the pavement was Morgan Jones, of No. 4 Piccadilly, Cheapside, Islington. He died in the reign of Richard III, of the prevailing disorder. An ax fell on his neck. The coloring of the pavement is very beautiful, and will immediately attract the notice of the visitor. Part of it is white and the other part black. The part that is white has been washed. This was done upon the occasion of the coronation of George II, and the person who did it was knighted, as the reader will already have opined. The iron railings cannot be too much admired. They were designed and constructed by Ralph Benson, of No. 9 Grace Church Street, Fen Church Street, Upper Terrace, Tottenham Court Road, Felter Lane, London, C. E., by special appointment blacksmith to His Royal Majesty, George III, of gracious memory, and were done at his own shop, by his own hands, and under his own personal supervision. Relics of this great artist's inspiration are exceedingly rare, and are valued at enormous sums; however, two shovels and a horseshoe made by him are on file at the British Museum, and no stranger should go away from London without seeing them. One of the shovels is undoubtedly genuine, but all authorities agree that the other one is spurious. It is not known which is the spurious one, and this is unfortunate, for nothing connected with this great man can be deemed of trifling importance. It is said that he was buried at Westminster Abbey, but was taken up and hanged in chains at Tyburn at the time of the Restoration, under the impression that he was Cromwell. But this is considered doubtful, by some, because he was not yet born at the time of the Restoration. The railings are nine feet three inches high, from the top of the stone pediment to the spearheads that form the apex, and twelve feet four inches high from the ground to the apex, the stone pediment being three feet one inch high, all of solid stone. The railings are not merely stood up on the pediment, but are mortised in, in the most ravishing manner. It was originally intended to make the railings two inches higher than they are, but the idea was finally abandoned, for some reason or other. This is greatly to be regretted, because it makes the fence out of proportion to the rest of Saint Paul's, and seriously mars the general effect. The spearheads upon the tops of the railings were gilded upon the death of Henry VIII, out of respect for the memory of that truly great King. The artist who performed the work was knighted by the regency, and hanged by Queen Mary when she came into power. * * *

The stone pediment upon which the iron railings stand was designed and erected by William Marlow, of 14 Threadneedle Street, Paternoster Row, St. Gile's, Belgravia, W. C., and is composed of alternate layers of rock, one above the other, and all cemented together in the most compact and impressive manner. The style of its architecture is a combination of the Pre-Raphaelite and the Renaissance—just enough of the Pre-Raphaelite to make it firm and substantial, and just enough of the Renaissance to impart to the whole a calm and gracious expression. There is nothing like this stone wall in England. We have no such artists nowadays. To find true art, we must go back to the past. Let the visitor note the tone of this wall, and the feeling. No work of art can be intelligently and enjoyably contemplated unless you know about tone and feeling, and can tell at a glance which is the tone and which is the feeling—and can talk about it with the guidebook shut up. I will venture to say that there is more tone in that stone wall than was ever hurled into a stone wall before; and as for feeling, it is just suffocated with it. As a whole, this fence is absolutely without its equal. If Michael Angelo could have seen this fence, would he have wasted his years sitting on a stone worshiping the cathedral of Florence? No; he would have spent his life gazing at this fence, and he would have taken a wax impression of it with him when he died. Michael Angelo and I may be considered extravagant, but as for me, if you simply mention art, I cannot be calm. I can go down on my knees before one of those decayed and venerable old masters that you have to put a sign on to tell which side of it you are looking at, and I do not want any bread, I do not want any meat, I do not want any air to breathe—I can *live* in the tone and the feeling of it. Expression—expression is the thing—in art. I do not care what it expresses, and I cannot most always sometimes tell, generally, but expression is what I worship, it is what I glory in, with all my impetuous nature. All the traveling world are just like me.

Marlow, the architect and builder of the stone pediment I was speaking of, was the favorite pupil of the lamented Hugh Miller, and worked in the same quarry with him. Specimens of the stone, for the cabinet, can be easily chipped off by the tourist with his hammer, in the customary way. I will observe that the stone was brought from a quarry on the Surrey side, near London. You can go either by Blackfriars Bridge, or Westminster Bridge or the Thames tunnel—fare, two shillings in a cab. It is best seen at sunrise, though many prefer moonlight.

The front yard of Saint Paul's is just like the back yard, except that it is adorned with a very noble and imposing statue of a black woman, which is said to have resembled Queen Anne, in some respects. It is five feet four inches high from the top of the figure to the pedestal, and nine feet seven inches from the top of the figure to the ground, the pedestal being four feet three inches high—all of solid stone. The figure measures eleven inches around the arm, and fifty-three inches around the body. The rigidity of the drapery has been much admired.

I will not make any description of the rest of Old Saint Paul's, for that has already been done in every book upon

London that has thus far been written, and therefore the reader must be measurably familiar with it. My only object is to instruct the reader upon matters which have been strangely neglected by other tourists, and if I have supplied a vacuum which must often have been painfully felt, my reward is sufficient. I have endeavored to furnish the exact dimensions of everything in feet and inches, in the customary exciting way, and likewise to supply names and dates and gushings upon art which will instruct the future tourist how to feel and what to think, and how to tell it when he gets home.

Artemus Ward
The Tower of London 1866

MR PUNCH, MY DEAR SIR, I skurcely need inform you that your excellent Tower is very pop'lar with peple from the agricultooral districks, and it was chiefly them class which I found waitin at the gates the other mornin.

I saw at once that the Tower was established on a firm basis. In the entire history of firm basisis I don't find a basis more firmer than this one.

"You have no Tower in America?" said a man in the crowd, who had somehow detected my denomination.

"Alars! no," I anserd; "we boste of our enterprise and improovements, and yit we are devoid of a Tower. America, oh my onhappy country! thou hast not got no Tower! It's a sweet Boon."

The gates was opened after awhile, and we all purchist tickets, and went into a waitin-room.

"My frens," said a pale-faced little man, in black close, "this is a sad day."

"Inasmuch as to how?" I said.

"I mean it is sad to think that so many peple have been killed within these gloomy walls. My frens, let us drop a tear!"

"No," I said, "you must excuse me. Others may drop one if they feel like it; but as for me, I decline. The early managers of this institootion were a bad lot, and their crimes were trooly orful; but I can't sob for those who died four or five hundred years ago. If they was my oan relations I couldn't. It's absurd to shed sobs over things which occurd durin the rain of Henry the Three. Let us be cheerful," I continnerd. "Look at the festiv Warders, in their red flannil jackets. They are cheerful, and why should it not be thusly with us?"

A Warder now took us in charge, and showed us the Trater's Gate, the armers, and things. The Trater's Gate is wide enuft to admit about twenty traters abrest, I should jedge; but beyond this, I couldn't see that it was superior to gates in gen'ral.

Traters, I will here remark, are a onfornit class of peple. If they wasn't, they wouldn't be traters. They conspire to bust up a country—they fail, and they're traters. They bust her, and they become statesmen and heroes.

Take the case of Gloster, afterwards Old Dick the Three, who may be seen at the Tower on horseback, in a heavy tin overcoat—take Mr Gloster's case. Mr. G. was a conspirator of the basist dye, and if he'd failed, he would have been hung on a sour apple tree. But Mr G. succeeded, and became great. He was slewd by Col. Richmond, but he lives in histry, and his equestrian figger may be seen daily for a sixpence, in conjunction with other em'nent persons, and no extra charge for the Warder's able and bootiful lectur. * * *

The Warder shows us some instroments of tortur, such as thumbscrews, throat-collars, &c., statin that these was conkered from the Spanish Armady, and addin what a crooil peple the Spaniards was in them days—which elissited from a bright-eyed little girl of about twelve summers the remark that she tho't it *was* rich to talk about the crooilty of the Spaniards usin thumbscrews, when we was in a Tower where so many poor peple's heads had been cut off. This made the Warder stammer and turn red.

I was so pleased with the little girl's brightness that I could have kissed the dear child, and I would if she'd been six years older.

I think my companions intended makin a day of it, for they all had sandwiches, sassiges, etc. The sad-lookin man, who had wanted us to drop a tear afore we started to go round, fling'd such quantities of sassige into his mouth that I expected to see him choke hisself to death; he said to me, in the Beauchamp Tower, where the poor prisoners writ their onhappy names on the cold walls, "This is a sad sight."

"It is, indeed," I anserd. "You're black in the face. You shouldn't eat sassige in public without some rehearsals beforehand. You manage it orkwardly."

"No," he said, "I mean this sad room."

Indeed, he was quite right. Tho' so long ago all these drefful things happened, I was very glad to git away from this gloomy room, and go where the rich and sparklin Crown Jewils is kept. I was so pleased with the Queen's Crown, that it occurd to me what a agree'ble surprise it would be to send a sim'lar one home to my wife; and I asked the Warder what was the vally of a good, well-constructed Crown like that. He told me, but on cypherin up with a pencil the amount of funs I have in the Jint Stock Bank, I conclooded I'd send her a genteel silver watch instid.

And so I left the Tower. It is a solid and commandin edifis, but I deny that it is cheerful. I bid it adoo without a pang.

Mark Twain
The British Museum 1872

I (UPON RECOMMENDATION of two householders of London) am provided with a ticket to the Reading Room, and this is always open, whereas the rest of the Museum is only open three days in the week.

What a place it is!

Mention some very rare curiosity of a peculiar nature— a something which you have read about somewhere but never seen—they show you a dozen! They show you all the possible varieties of that thing! They show you curiously wrought and jeweled necklaces of beaten gold worn by the ancient Egyptians, Assyrians, Etruscans, Greeks, Britons—every people, of the forgotten ages, indeed. They show you the ornaments of all the tribes and peoples that live or ever did live. Then they show you a cast taken from Cromwell's face in death; then the venerable vase that once contained the ashes of Xerxes; then you drift into some other room and stumble upon a world of the flint hatchets of prehistoric days; and reindeer-horn handles; and pieces of bone with figures of animals delicately carved upon them; and long rows of bone fishhooks and needles of the period—everything, indeed, connected with the household economy of the cave and lake dwellers—and every object too, so repeated, and multiplied, and remultiplied that they suddenly whisk away your doubts and you find yourself accepting as a fact that these implements and ornaments are not scattered accidents, but deliberately designed and tediously wrought, and in very common use in some queer age of the world or other. And the fact that many of them are found in ruined habitations in the bottoms of Swiss lakes, and many in caverns in other parts of Europe (buried under slowly created and very thick layers of limestone), does not encourage one to try to claim these parties as very recent kin. And then you pass along and perhaps you ask if they have got such a thing as a mummy about their clothes—and bless your heart and they rush you into a whole Greenwood Cemetery of them—old mummies, young mummies, he mummies, she mummies, high-toned mummies, ragged mummies, old slouches, mummies in good whole coffins, mummies on the half-shell, mummies with money, mummies that are "busted," kings and emperors, loafers and bummers, all straightened out as comfortable and happy in a Christian museum as if they had brought their knitting with them and this was the very hotel they had been hunting for, for four thousand years and upwards. And while you are wondering if these defunct had human feelings, human sympathies, human emotions like your own, you turn pensively about and find an eloquent answer: an Egyptian woman's enormous chignon and the box she carried it in when she went out to a party! You want to kiss that poor old half-bushel of curled and plaited hair; you want to uncover the glass case and shed some tears on it. You recognize the fact that in the old, old times, woman was the same quaint, fascinating, eccentric muggins she is in these.

Willard Price
An Amazing Labyrinth 1958

WE WALKED THROUGH the magnificent gardens [of Hampton Court] to the Maze. Now I had a particular reason for wanting to take Mary through the Maze. I knew the code and she didn't know that I knew it. Before we had left America I had come upon it in the *Encyclopædia Britannica* and had memorized it. She would certainly be impressed when I would lead her through the labyrinth without a moment of hesitation and she would say I was wonderful, and I would say it was nothing, just a sixth sense.

We paid our threepence apiece and entered the narrow passage between high hedges. We came to a passage leading both left and right and I confidently turned right. That was what the code had said, always turn right. Or was it left? Anyhow we went on, my wife's amazement growing as we swept around every corner without a moment's pause for thought. Other people stood about debating, arguing, complaining, but we forged ahead at full speed.

The Maze is not large and with luck you should not have to go more than a hundred yards or so to reach the center, a round place with benches where you may rest, then the same distance to get out. After we had gone about half a mile my wife showed signs of flagging. I was beginning to have a few doubts myself.

"I'm tired," Mary said. "Suppose we give it up?"

"Just a little farther and we'll come to the center. You can sit down there and rest."

A half-mile more. Then we dragged to a halt and looked at each other.

"Let's go back," Mary suggested. "Do you know the way out?"

"Well, I think so."

If you kept to the right on the way in you would keep to the left going out. We kept to the left and in five minutes walked into the center. This surprised my wife, but I pointed out that it was just what I had been trying to do all the time.

We rested while I pondered. The code must have said left, not right. Then going out you would keep to the right, not left.

We took to the trail again, keeping always to the right. In five minutes we were back in the center. It was getting dark now. We were hungry. The other visitors had gone, or had died of exhaustion somewhere in the labyrinth. A cold rain was beginning to fall.

I shouted. No answer. Had the gatekeeper gone home? We both shouted, but without effect. I picked up a pebble and threw it. If it happened to crack the pate of a gatekeeper I didn't much care. But it brought no curse, no sound at all. More stones, and more shouts.

Then a beautiful sight. A guard appeared on a high platform just outside the Maze.

"All out," he called. "Closing time."

"Which way?" I inquired.

"I'll come in and get you."

He led us out. To save our face he said kindly: "Of course I know you could get out by yourselves, but that might take longer and it's time to close."

I let it go at that.

Later I saw the code, this time not in the *Encyclopædia Britannica* but in the tourist magazine, *Coming Events*. Here it is, but don't try to carry it in your memory. Paste it in your hat.

Og tfel no gniretne dna neht no eht tsrif owt snoisacco erehw ereht si na noitpo og thgir. Retfa taht peek ot eht tfel.

H. V. Morton
The Isle of London 1935

I THOUGHT, IN MY VANITY, that I knew London.
I realize now that no one understands London until he has explored the significant chasms of this white island, this mother of London. How would you analyze the beauty of London? Surely it is due to the changefulness of this island stone that gathers smoke shadows on its windless side as trees gather lichen. On dull days it looms, remote and gray, as if withdrawn into some region of thoughtfulness, and in the sunlight it blazes in sudden

whiteness, so that you feel London has as many moods as a woman.

Somerset House, St. Paul's, the Bank, the Royal Exchange, the Mansion House, the Law Courts, the British Museum, all the Wren churches—one could extend the list to the end of the chapter—have left their caves, gullies, and gaps in the Isle of Portland. What an unforgettable experience it is to walk in the mighty bed from which, at the command of Wren, St. Paul's arose to stand guard on Ludgate Hill.

As I walked along the dusty roads of the island, which dazzle the eyes like snow in sunlight, I thought not only of the buildings which Portland has already given to London but of the London to be which we will never walk, that slumbers still in darkness in the womb of this pregnant Isle. There is a new Bank of England there. They will be cutting it out of the hills soon. There are new streets there. I had the queer fancy that perhaps my footsteps might echo down to the London of tomorrow, stirring it from its prehistoric slumbers, giving it an uneasy nightmare of destiny.

And this I thought: that never again will I look on London with quite the same eyes. Always at the back of my mind will be, as I walk the streets of London, knowledge of a white island lying out to sea like a great whale. When I see Portland stone in London I shall think of the sea breaking against high hills; I shall hear the scream of the gulls; the suck back of pebbles on the little stony beaches; the white dust lying over the road in the little mysterious Isle of London.

H. Allen Smith
The Scribblers' London 1952

JUDGING FROM THE GUIDEBOOKS, the major heroes of historic London are not the kings but the writers. If Samuel Johnson paused in an alleyway to fondle another cat, the date and the precise location are set down in the books; if Samuel Pepys stopped in a garden to fondle another lady's bosom, that incident, too, is recorded. The places these people lived, the places where they drank or danced or worshiped, are indicated on the maps and described in the books. Almost the whole of London is a monument to Dickens and the localities associated with him personally are visited and revered; more than that, the localities associated with his fictional characters are even more celebrated. Many Dickens admirers are more interested in standing before the site of an inn where David Copperfield stayed overnight, or where Mr. Pickwick first met Sam Weller, than they are in looking at the residence of Dickens himself. The giants of the London scene, in almost every era, have been the scribblers and their names dominate the books that have been written about the metropolis—Pepys and Johnson and Dickens, as mentioned, and Sheridan, Macaulay, Byron, Thackeray, Tennyson, Chaucer, Keats, Shelley, Gibbon, Browne, Sterne, Swift, Shaw, Lamb, Boswell, Addison, Goldsmith, Carlyle and Edgar Wallace.

This is all a lot of nonsense of course. In America we know writers for what they are—insufferable troublemakers. Unless he can catch a lot of fish like Ernest Hemingway, a man who writes in America is a man incapable of making an honest living, a pantywaist sort of person indulging in a profession that is close kin to working in needlepoint, rug-hookery and crying at weddings.

When I applied for my passport in New York I made a mistake by identifying myself as a writer. Where other people with respectable occupations were pushed through in a hurry, I was cross-examined at some length. I had to go out and get letters from well-bred horse traders in the business community to show that I am not a bolshevik, a Luddite, a Technocrat, an Anabaptist, a Bevanite or a typhoid carrier. In the end I convinced them that I don't believe in anything, and am therefore safe.

To round off the sightseeing portion of this chapter, Stephen Leacock will give us his overall impression of the sights London has to offer. Since Dr. Leacock never ever takes the close and narrow route—not to mention an occasional boulevard—since even the wild goose is not prey enough for him, be sure to hold on tight.

Stephen Leacock
Impressions of London 1922

LONDON, THE NAME OF WHICH is already known to millions of readers of this book, is beautifully situated on the river Thames, which here sweeps in a wide curve with much the same breadth and majesty as the St. Jo River at South Bend, Indiana. London, like South Bend itself, is a city of clean streets and admirable side-walks and has an excellent water supply. One is at once struck by the number of excellent and well-appointed motor-cars that one sees on every hand, the neatness of the shops, and the cleanliness and cheerfulness of the faces of the people. In short, as an English writer said of Peterborough, Ontario, there is a distinct note of optimism in the air. I forget who it was who said this, but, at any rate, I have been in Peterborough myself and have seen it.

Contrary to my expectations and contrary to all our Transatlantic precedent, I was *not* met at the depot by one of the leading citizens, himself a member of the Municipal Council, driving his own motor-car. He did *not* tuck a fur rug about my knees, present me with a really excellent cigar, and proceed to drive me about the town so as to show me the leading points of interest—the municipal reservoir, the gasworks, and the municipal *abattoir*. In fact, he was not there. But I attribute his absence not to any lack of hospitality, but merely to a certain reserve in the English character. They are as yet unused to the arrival of lecturers. When they get to be more accustomed to their coming, they will learn to take them straight to the municipal *abattoir,* just as we do.

For lack of better guidance, therefore, I had to form my impressions of London by myself. In the mere physical sense there is much to attract the eye. The city is able to boast of many handsome public buildings and offices which compare favourably with anything on the other side of the Atlantic. On the bank of the Thames itself rises the power house of the Westminster Electric Supply Corporation, a handsome modern edifice in the later Japanese style. Close by are the commodious premises of the Imperial Tobacco Company, while at no great distance the Chelsea Gas Works add a striking feature of rotundity. Passing northward, one observes Westminster Bridge, notable as a principal station of the Underground Railway. This station and the one next above it, the Charing Cross one, are connected by a wide thoroughfare called Whitehall. One of the best American drug stores is here situated. The upper end of Whitehall opens into the majestic and spacious Trafalgar Square. Here are grouped in imposing proximity the offices of the Canadian Pacific and other railways, the International Sleeping Car Company, the Montreal *Star,* and the Anglo-Dutch Bank. Two of the best American barber shops are conveniently grouped near the Square, while the existence of a tall stone monument in the middle of the Square itself enables the American visitor to find them without difficulty. Passing eastward towards the heart of the City, one notes on the left hand the imposing pile of St. Paul's, an enormous church with a round dome on the top, suggesting strongly the first Church of Christ (Scientist) on Euclid Avenue, Cleveland. But, the English churches not being labelled, the visitor is often at a loss to distinguish them.

A little further on one finds oneself in the heart of financial London. Here all the great financial institutions of America—The First National Bank of Milwaukee, The Planters' National Bank of St. Louis, The Montana Farmers Trust Co., and many others—have either their offices or their agents. The Bank of England, which acts as the London Agent of the Montana Farmers Trust Company, and the London County Bank, which represents the People's Deposit Co., of Yonkers, N.Y., are said to be in the neighbourhood.

This particular part of London is connected with the existence of that strange and mysterious thing called "the City." I am still unable to decide whether the City is a person, or a place, or a thing. But as a form of being I give it credit for being the most emotional, the most volatile, the most peculiar creature in the world. You read in the morning paper that the City is "deeply depressed." At noon it is reported that the City is "buoyant," and by four o'clock that the City is "wildly excited." * * *

A little beyond the City and further down the river the visitor finds this district of London terminating in the gloomy and forbidding Tower, the principal penitentiary of the City. Here Queen Victoria was imprisoned for many years.

Excellent gasoline can be had at the American Garage immediately north of the Tower, where motor repairs of all kinds are also carried on.

These, however, are but the superficial pictures of London, gathered by the eye of the tourist. A far deeper meaning is found in the examination of the great historic monuments of the City. The principal ones of these are the Tower of London (just mentioned), the British Museum, and Westminster Abbey. No visitor to London should fail to see these. Indeed, he ought to feel that his visit to England is wasted unless he has seen them. I speak strongly on the point because I feel strongly on it. To my mind there is something about the grim fascination of the historic Tower, the cloistered quiet of the Museum, and the majesty of the ancient Abbey which will make it the regret of my life that I didn't see any one of the three. I fully meant to, but I failed; and I can only hope that the circumstances of my failure may be helpful to other visitors.

The Tower of London I most certainly intended to inspect. Each day, after the fashion of every tourist, I wrote for myself a little list of things to do, and I always put the Tower of London on it. No doubt the reader knows the kind of little list that I mean. It runs:

1. *Go to bank.*
2. *Buy a shirt.*
3. *National Gallery.*
4. *Razor blades.*
5. *Tower of London.*
6. *Soap.*

The itinerary, I regret to say, was never carried out in full. I was able at times both to go to the bank and buy a shirt in a single morning; at other times I was able to buy razor blades and almost to find the National Gallery. Meantime I was urged on all sides by my London acquaintances not to fail to see the Tower. "There's a grim fascination about the place," they said, "you mustn't miss it." I am quite certain that in due course of time I should have made my way to the Tower but for the fact that I made a fatal discovery. I found out that the London people who urged me to go and see the Tower had never seen it themselves. It appears they never go near it. One night at a dinner a man next to me said, "Have you seen the Tower? You really ought to. There's a grim fascination about it." I looked him in the face. "Have you seen it yourself?" I asked. "Oh, yes," he answered. "I've seen it." "When?" I asked. The man hesitated. "When I was just a boy," he said, "my father took me there." "How long ago is that?" I inquired. "About forty years ago," he answered. "I always mean to go again, but I don't somehow seem to get the time."

After this I got to understand that when a Londoner says, "Have you seen the Tower of London?" the answer is, "No, and neither have you."

Take the parallel case of the British Museum. Here is a place that is a veritable treasure house. A repository of some of the most priceless historical relics to be found upon the earth. It contains, for instance, the famous Papyrus Manuscript of Totmes II of the first Egyptian dynasty—a thing known to scholars all over the world as the oldest extant specimen of what can be called writing; indeed, one can here see the actual evolution (I am quoting from a work of reference, or at least from my recollection of it) from the ideographic cuneiform to the phonetic syllabic script. Every time I have read about that manuscript and have happened to be in Orillia (Ontario) or Schenectady (N.Y.), or any such place, I have felt that I would be willing to take a whole trip to England to have five minutes at the British Museum, just five, to look at that papyrus. Yet as soon as I got to London this changed. The railway stations of London have been so arranged that to get to any train for the north or west, the traveller must pass the British Museum. The first time I went by it in a taxi I felt quite a thrill. "Inside those walls," I thought to myself, "is the manuscript of Totmes II." The next time I actually stopped the taxi. "Is that the British Museum?" I asked the driver. "I think it is something of the sort, sir," he said. I hesitated. "Drive me," I said, "to where I can buy safety razor blades."

After that I was able to drive past the Museum with the quiet assurance of a Londoner, and to take part in dinner-table discussions as to whether the British Museum or the Louvre contains the greater treasures. It is quite easy, any way. All you have to do is to remember that the Winged Victory of Samothrace is in the Louvre, and the papyrus of Totmes II (or some such document) is in the Museum.

The Abbey, I admit, is indeed majestic. I did not intend to miss going into it. But I felt, as so many tourists have, that I wanted to enter it in the proper frame of mind. I never got into the frame of mind; at least, not when near the Abbey itself. I have been in exactly that frame of mind when on State Street, Chicago, or on King Street, Toronto, or anywhere three thousand miles away from the Abbey. But by bad luck I never struck both the frame of mind and the Abbey at the same time.

But the Londoners, after all, in not seeing their own wonders, are only like the rest of the world. The people who live in Buffalo never go to see the Niagara Falls; people in Cleveland don't know which is Mr. Rockefeller's house; and people live and even die in New York without going up to the top of the Woolworth Building. And, anyway, the past is remote and the present is near. I know a cab driver in the city of Quebec whose business in life it is to drive people up to see the Plains of Abraham, but, unless they bother him to do it, he doesn't show them the spot where Wolfe fell. What he does point out with real zest is the place where the Mayor and the City Council sat on the wooden platform that they put up for the municipal celebration last summer.

Food. English food. Most of the humor on English food is just what you would expect: biting, voracious, sour as the stomachs of those who partake of it. So we have decided to spare you. There's no reason to add insult to injury. As at least one member of each parental unit says, "If you don't have something nice to say...."

English shopping is far better than English cooking, but it has little to do with tourism. It may get us there, but it's not like we buy mainly souvenirs. No, for us it's dresses and jackets and the unisex kilt; china and materials; books and records. What really stands out, as we scour the department stores and boutiques, is how many of them cater to the Queen. She comes to appear not the grand woman and symbol of the greatness of Britain, but a human vacuum cleaner who consumes and consumes and consumes.

Just to show you it's nothing personal, nothing new, here's American travel writer J. M. Bailey telling us the state of the stores in 1879, when the Queen was named Victoria. And then the outrageous Art Buchwald takes us from the most fashionable stores of London into the midst of the greatest royal gathering of the year, short of a marriage: the horse races at Ascot.

J. M. Bailey
By Special Appointment 1879

EVERY OTHER STORE PROMINENTLY announces the fact that it is doing business by "special appointment to H. M. the Queen," or "to H. R. H. the Prince of Wales."

Feeling an unquenchable longing one afternoon to see the Queen, I stepped into a shoe-store which announced itself as attending to her shodding, and waited very patiently for an hour for her to call in "to see if that shoe was fixed;" but I did not see her. "By special appointment," &c., has stared me in the face at every turn; but I bore it uncomplainingly until I saw over a stovepipe-hat-store the announcement, "By special appointment to H. M. the Queen."

Then I caved.

By a careful and unbiassed calculation, I learn that there are at present, administering to the various needs of Queen Victoria, 11,000 grocers, 2,150 stationers, 8,093 dry-goods merchants, 1,608 tinners, 16,040 butchers, 1,100 jewellers, 3,840 tobacconists, 243 hatters, 1,240 carriage-makers, 26,432 miscellaneous.

No wonder the country is in debt. But business is stimulated.

Art Buchwald
Ordeal at Ascot 1954

I KNOW IT'S POOR FORM to brag when one is in England, but when one goes to Ascot one likes to make a point of it. Ascot, for the uninitiated, is the only race-course in England which belongs to the Crown. Founded by Good Queen Anne in 1711, Royal Ascot Week is the most important event on the social horseflesh calendar. Any blue-blooded Briton will tell you a visit to Ascot during Royal Ascot Week is "the thing to do."

But one doesn't just go to Ascot—one worries oneself sick making preparations for it. Rumor has it that Ascot is so exclusive that it is the only racecourse in the world where the horses own the people. One must be dressed to the teeth when one is in attendance. The only attire acceptable is the gray topper, the cutaway morning coat, the half-inch-striped trousers, the four-buttoned gray waistcoat, the starched collar, gray neckwear and, of course, the tightly wrapped, smartly packed black umbrella.

No one knows the historical significance behind each of these pieces of clothing. There is a story that the gray toppers can be traced back to early races at Ascot when people carried rabbits in their hats to the track. (Some say that before the horse evolved to its present shape, it looked like a big rabbit and, during the early years at Ascot, the only animals that raced were rabbits who chased greyhound dogs around a circular track.)

But so much for history. One doesn't buy a cutaway suit in London, one hires it at Moss Bros. (pronounced Maws Braws). Moss Bros. is to the suit-hire business what Lloyd's is to the insurance business. From Ascot to Lord's to Eton to Harrow to the Royal Garden Parties and society weddings, Moss Bros. hire-suits are on parade.

When I went to Moss Bros. to hire mine, I found fourteen men in front of me. A straw poll revealed that most of us were for Ascot, though two admitted to the Eton-Harrow cricket match and one said the Royal Garden Party. The clerk who took care of me said that the suit he was letting me have had seen service at two horse shows, a Coronation, one Westminster baptism, a flower show at Sussex and a wedding which brought together two of Great Britain's leading families. The suit had never been to Ascot before, but the clerk was confident it would, like every Moss Bros. suit, do its duty. The cost for complete hire was £3.10 per day.

The only question which presented itself was whether I should wear the backless waistcoat or not. The clerk said, "We never like to interfere in these matters, but the naked-shoulder-blade model is coming into its own and you would be perfectly correct in wearing it. I know this may sound rather daring, but at times one must be courageous."

It was one of those decisions one hates to make. I searched my conscience and finally decided to throw caution to the wind. I would wear the naked-shoulder-blade model in spite of everybody. When it comes to fashion I've always been known as a pace setter.

After hiring the morning coat, the naked-shoulder-blade waistcoat and the striped trousers, I procured an umbrella and strode out to Hyde Park for a dress rehearsal. There I was shocked to discover that there are very few Englishmen who know anything about umbrellas. It happened this way. There was a dry spell of about five minutes during London's famed inclement weather and I was doing my best to roll up my umbrella when a dapper man wearing a derby, a starched collar and an old school tie stopped and said, "I beg your pardon. You seem to be a stranger here and, if you don't mind my saying so, you're making a muck-up of that umbrella."

I looked a little hurt.

"Oh, forgive me for not introducing myself. My name is Gerald Spokes and I'm a member of the Royal Umbrella and Parasol Society, an organizatin devoted to correcting the mishandling of umbrellas in the British Isles."

"The mishandling of umbrellas?"

"Yes. You see, most of the great umbrella men have died out and the art of sporting an umbrella is fast disappearing. Our society sends out voluntary members to give instructions—free of charge, of course—in order to correct these flagrant violations of proper umbrella taste and decency. Would you care to have some instruction?"

I said I'd be very happy to receive some.

"Good. Now the first thing you must learn is the nomenclature. There is the point at the bottom. Then there is the mainmast which runs up and meets the clutch, or handle. Just before the mainmast is the control button where you open or close the umbrella and there are the ribs and the pleated silk. Each piece of the umbrella plays its own important part, and without any one of them the whole instrument could easily sag or fall to pieces.

"Your umbrella is not badly built, though it is a little racy for this late in the afternoon. Malacca handles such as yours are preferred before four o'clock. But being an American, I don't imagine anyone will bother you about it.

"Now I noticed, while I was watching you before, that you twirled your umbrella. Sir, I can't impress upon you enough what bad taste this is. An occasional twirl in early morning is tolerated, but never, never in the afternoon!

"You were also using your umbrella as a cane. Even if you had a bad limp, which you don't seem to have, it is against all decent propriety to use your umbrella as a cane. It must be carried with your gloves one inch from your body and draped over your left arm exactly six inches from the wrist bone, the open part of the handle or clutch facing in. And you must be careful that the umbrella does not swing more than ten degrees in any direction.

"So far so good. The next question is, what is an umbrella good for? The most important use for an umbrella is, of course, for hailing taxicabs. But there are so few of us who know how to hail a taxi in the correct manner. Let me show you.

"Stand with your feet about nine inches apart, firmly planted on the sidewalk. Take the umbrella from its left-arm circling position and bring it over across your chest. Then, in one motion, raise it so that the forearm is at a forty-five-degree angle to the body and that there is no daylight between the arm and the side of the body.

"Do not wave your arm and do not make a thrust at a taxi. You may flip some taxi meters by mistake and there will be the devil to pay. The only time to extend your arm is when some bounder stations himself in front of you and tries to steal your cab. Then raise the umbrella, full length from the body, to ninety degrees and clout him over the head.

"The umbrella can also be used to acknowledge a greeting, but only with another man. You still have to tip your derby to a woman, and if you wave and tip at the same time you may trip yourself up.

"Another important use for the umbrella is for rapping on doors, which is far preferable to ringing a bell. In such cases you grip the umbrella in the center at the balance point and, moving the wrist up and down, you rap rap rap with the handle. If there is no answer you can always use the umbrella to open a transom and climb in that way.

"The umbrella has very important investigating properties and is particularly valuable in a park for poking paper lunch bags that might still have some food in them, and also for poking under rocks for fishing worms.

"I wish to point out one more thing. You never roll an umbrella when it's wet, and you always roll from the bottom up, making sure the ribs are locked and the silken pleats are equidistant before you secure the button."

I thanked Mr. Spokes very much.

"Don't thank me, thank the Royal Umbrella and Parasol Society. And now, if you'll excuse me, I must hail a taxi."

Mr. Spokes crossed his right arm over, gripped the handle firmly and in one movement brought it across his chest smartly at a 45-degree angle. It was a beautiful maneuver and there was no daylight showing between the arm and the side of the body.

After receiving this invaluable drill in proper umbrella usage, I went over to Fortnum and Mason, the food store, and ordered a hamper for the day. Tradition demands that during Royal Ascot you either eat in the Royal Enclosure, or at the White Club tent, or next to your car in the parking lot with a food hamper from Fortnum and Mason.

The clerk told me Royal Ascot called for lobster, chicken and tongue, potato salad, cheese, peaches and champagne. He told me the hamper should be placed about four feet from the rear door of the car and eaten at least forty-five minutes before the first race. The hamper cost me three pounds ten, including the bottle of champagne.

There was only one more matter to be attended to—the question of the Royal Enclosure. It seems that the place to be at Ascot is the Royal Enclosure, where the Queen and five hundred selected people are located. It is so exclusive that up to this year no divorced persons were allowed in the enclosure, even to get a glimpse of the horses. But this time I heard that the barriers had been let down and divorced persons were being allowed in. Although it was tough on my wife, I immediately went out and got a divorce. So there I was, dressed in a Moss Bros. cutaway suit with the naked-shoulder-blade waistcoat, provisioned by Fortnum and Mason and completely divorced from my wife, going hick lickety split to Ascot. Jamaica Racetrack was never like this.

Suddenly my Rolls-Royce stopped going hick lickety split and went awr, mawr, gawr. Since Ascot Week is a royal week, under royal patronage, it wasn't surprising that I got into one of the most royal traffic jams of all time. The two-mile road from Windsor to Ascot was crowded with cars, bumper to bumper, and people, topper to topper. Everybody and his Lord High Chamberlain were off to the races, and it was only by a miracle that I managed to arrive in time for the first engagement. (It cost a quid to park, which shows you what kind of layout Ascot is.)

Taking my hamper in my right hand and my umbrella in the left hand I surged forth with the multitude.

Ascot is divided into many little islands of society. Besides the Royal Enclosure, there are the Paddock, where the horses mingle freely with the people; Tattersalls, where the bookmakers make book; the Silver Ring, where people known as the Ascot Snobs maintain boxes; the heath, where the commoners stand; and a Crèche, complete with sand pit, where children play while their parents watch the tote boards.

I first tried to get into the Royal Enclosure, but I was rudely turned away. I produced my divorce papers and the deposit slip on my cutaway suit from Moss Bros., but the guards would not admit me. It seemed a shabby way to treat someone from across the seas.

I took my hamper to the paddock and started to spread my lunch on the grass. Someone with an Ascot Authority badge approached me. "I'm sorry, you can't picnic here. The grass is reserved for the horses."

"But," I protested, "I paid three quid and ten bob for this hamper and I'm hungry."

"Sorry, sir," he replied. "Hampers are not permitted. We provide food at the track. Why don't you go over to one of the refreshment stands and have some jellied eels?"

"Some jellied what?"

"Eels, sir. They're delicious. Now get along before we put you in the gaol."

"The what?"

"The gaol. That's where we put people who spread their hampers all over the nickety-nick grass."

Not wanting to go to the gaol, I packed up my hamper and went over to have some jellied eels. Jellied eels can be eaten with or without a pint. On my first try the eel started to drip (it was a hot day) and I caught the gravy in my gray topper. It was a mistake. A man in a cutaway suit approached me. He flashed a card. "I'm a Moss Bros. inspector. That's a very serious offense you have just committed. May I please see your deposit slip?"

I showed it to him and he wrote something on the back.

"Moss Bros. have ruled people off the course for far less than this. Since you are a foreigner we'll let you off with a warning. When eating jellied eels you let the gravy drip onto the grass."

I apologized and put the topper back on my head. The gravy ran down to my collar.

He took the deposit slip back again and wrote some more. "When one allows gravy to fall into one's gray topper, one does not put it back on the head again until it is emptied."

I took the tail of my morning coat and wiped off the gravy from my collar.

"No, no, no," he screamed in despair. "The tail of the coat is never used as a napkin."

I handed over the deposit slip.

"Now get on with you and mind your manners or I'll take the suit away from you right here on the track."

I walked away quickly before he found something else wrong.

The horses were in the paddock and everyone was jammed together looking at them. Unfortunately I had my umbrella in the ring and tripped one of the horses. A man from the Umbrella Authority grabbed me by the arm. "One does not use one's umbrella to trip the horses. One keeps one's umbrella on one's arm or leans on it at parade rest behind the right hip. If you don't know how to use an umbrella properly we'll see that you are forbidden ever to use it again."

The horse got up from the ground and I wiped off his flank with the tail of my tailcoat. When I looked up the inspector from Moss Bros. was standing right beside me.

Abashed by his watchful presence, I left the paddock with the still full Fortnum and Mason hamper. My collar had wilted a little from the heat and the jellied-eel gravy, but otherwise I was perfectly attired. I made once again for the Royal Enclosure, which had now filled up with flowered frocks, cutaway suits and black umbrellas. Just as I was approaching it, the same Moss Bros. inspector caught up with me and whispered through his teeth, "Straighten your topper, pull up your cravat, button up your waistcoat and look smart. Where do you think you are—at a Henley Boat Race?"

I straightened up, but he continued to lecture me. "Look at all those Moss Bros. cutaways out there. You don't see one topper out of line, and look at you. Even the stripes on your trousers are crooked. Now go about your business and be careful, or else it's back to the Strand for you."

Seeing a large crowd of spectators and Her Majesty walking in the midst of them, I wormed my way through the Royal Enclosure fence and waited patiently for somebody to introduce me. But when Her Majesty walked by, she looked the other way. One of the bystanders, seeing the tears in my eyes, said, "The Queen Mother and Princess Margaret are meeting people over in that crowd. Perhaps you will be presented to them." I rushed over, fought my way through, tearing my coat on a maharaja's diamond pin, and stood hopefully facing the Queen Mother and Princess Margaret. They walked right by.

"Try the Duke of Edinburgh," a man suggested. I ran over, pushed through a large gathering of ladies, and, waving my umbrella at the Duke, I smiled hopefully. The ladies were furious and pushed me back out of sight, tearing my waistcoat in the bargain.

As I got up from the ground, someone else said: "The Duchess of Kent and Princess Alexandra are over there." It was too late. They had already disappeared into the Royal Box.

I took my hamper to the edge of the field and spread it out.

The man from Moss Bros. jumped out from behind a tree. "There you are. Everyone has been talking about you. Look at you. Your coat is torn, your naked-shoulder-blade waistcoat is askew, you're missing your collar button. I've had enough. Give me the suit."

"Right here on the field?"

"You can go out the back gate. No one will see you."

I took off the coat, the waistcoat, the shirt, the tie and the pants. "Can I keep the topper until tomorrow, in case it rains?" I asked.

"All right, but you better wear it correctly."

I escaped out through the back gate before anybody could spot me. It was a fine Royal Ascot, even though I didn't meet anyone worth mentioning and they took away the suit. But it needed a cleaning anyway.

All these things that cost money—horse races, clothing, museums, sights—are fine and good. But there's nothing like a walk in a free London park—Hyde, Regent's, Richmond, Hampstead Heath perhaps—to make us feel like a good Scot... no, I mean, to make us feel good and healthy. Not only that, but as the great Czechoslovak writer Karel Capek shows us in the next, and final, piece of this section, the parks reflect the character of the English, especially to someone from the Continent.

Karel Capek
The English Park 1925

THE MOST BEAUTIFUL THINGS IN ENGLAND are, perhaps, its trees. Of course, the meadows and the policemen too, but most of all the trees, the spendidly broad-shouldered, ancient, generous, free, venerable, vast trees. The trees at Hampton Court, Richmond Park, Windsor, and I don't know where else besides. It's possible that these trees have had a great influence on Toryism in England. I think they preserve the aristocratic instincts, the historical sense, Conservatism, tariffs, golf, the House of Lords, and other odd and antique things. I should probably be a rabid Radical if I lived in the Street of the Iron Balconies or in the Street of the Grey Bricks, but sitting under an ancient oak tree in the park at Hampton Court I was seriously tempted to acknowledge the value of old things, the high mission of old trees, the harmonious comprehensiveness of tradition, and the legitimacy of esteem for everything that is strong enough to preserve itself for ages.

It seems that in England there are many such ancient trees; in nearly everything here, in the clubs, in the literature, in the homes, you can somehow feel the timber and foliage of aged, venerable, and fearfully solid trees. As a matter of fact, here you see nothing conspicuously new—except the Tube, and maybe that's why it's so ugly. Old trees and old things contain imps, eccentric and jocular sprites, as do the English. They too are enormously solemn, solid, and venerable; suddenly there is a sort of rumbling within them, they make a grotesque remark, a fork of pixie-like humor flies out of them, and then once again they have the solemn appearance of an old leather armchair.

I don't know why, but this sober England strikes me as the most fairylike and romantic of all the countries I've seen. Perhaps it's on account of the old trees. Or no, perhaps it's due to the lawns. It's due to the fact that here you walk across fields instead of on footpaths. We Continental people won't dare walk except on roads and paved paths; this certainly has a huge influence on the development of our minds. When I saw the first gentleman strolling across the lawn in the park at Hampton Court, I imagined that he was a creature from Fairyland, although he was wearing a top hat. I expected him to ride into Kingston on a stag or to begin dancing, or a gardener to come up and give him a good scolding. But nothing happened, and at last even I dared to make my way straight across the grass to an old oak. And nothing happened! Never have I had a feeling of such unrestricted liberty. It's very curious; here, evidently, man is not regarded as a obnoxious animal. Here, they don't subscribe to the dismal myth that grass won't grow beneath our hooves. Here, a man has the right to walk across the meadow as if he were a wood-nymph or a property owner. I think that this has a considerable influence upon his character and view of the world. It opens up the marvelous possibility of walking elsewhere than along a road, without regarding oneself as a beast of prey, a highwayman, or an anarchist.

"I understand the Danes and the Dutch and the Germans when they speak English. Why don't I understand the English?"

J. B. Handelsman

ᵉ⊷The English

ᵉ⊷*The English. They're some kinda people. A far, far out-post of the Roman Empire made up of savages who painted themselves blue (and many still do, at least their hair), somehow they managed to soak up the peoples, languages, and customs that came the furthest from wherever they were going—at least before they went and crossed the ocean and found further and further places to go. But who is less far-out than the English? A people who, via the unyielding lust of a king and the unyielding virginity of a queen, managed both to break from Rome and the rest of the continent and to build a navy that would lead them to the most far-flung empire ever. A people who led the world, kicking and screaming (and those were just the foremen), into the Industrial Age, through both scientific and economic inventions inconceivable elsewhere. A people so free they don't even put their constitution in writing, yet they still queue up without a single squeal. What can you say? Well, here's a few humorists and travel writers who have a great deal to say.*

First, one of the most popular contemporary travel writers, Paul Theroux, on a few selected English ec-centricities. Then French humorist Pierre Daninos reflects on the Englishman's contradictory nature; philosopher George Santayana, a native of Spain, tells us why the lion and the unicorn together are the Briton's symbols; and Margaret Halsey skewers the Englishman conversing. Israeli humorist Ephraim Kishon shows us two of the many sides of English humor; and American

79

travel writer George W. Hills introduces us to the typical English landlady.

Paul Theroux
What They Do 1983

ONCE, FROM BEHIND A CLOSED DOOR, I heard an Englishwoman exclaim with real pleasure, "They are *funny*, the Yanks!" And I crept away and laughed to think that an English person was saying such a thing. And I thought: They wallpaper their ceilings! They put little knitted bobble-hats on their soft-boiled eggs to keep them warm! They don't give you bags in supermarkets! They say sorry when you step on their toes! Their government makes them get a hundred-dollar license every year for watching television! They issue drivers' licenses that are valid for thirty or forty years— mine expires in the year 2011! They charge you for matches when you buy cigarettes! They smoke on buses! They drive on the left! They spy for the Russians! They say "nigger" and "Jewboy" without flinching! They call their houses Holmleigh and Sparrow View! They sunbathe in their underwear! They don't say "You're welcome"! They still have milk bottles and milkmen, and junk-dealers with horse-drawn wagons! They love candy and Lucozade and leftovers called bubble-and-squeak! They live in Barking and Dorking and Shellow Bowells! They have amazing names, like Mr. Eatwell and Lady Inkpen and Major Twaddle and Miss Tosh! And they think *we're* funny?

Pierre Daninos
Contradictions 1957

THE ENGLISH CAN BE EXPLAINED by their Anglo-Saxon heritage and the influence of the Methodists. But I prefer to explain them in terms of tea, roast beef, and rain. A people is first of all what it eats, drinks, and gets pelted with. Men who are ceaselessly battered by the wind and the rain and shrouded in a permanent fog end up themselves turning into raincoats which shed criticism as easily as an oilskin sheds water. Men who drink tea seven times a day and eat the same vegetables and meats all year round naturally end up with the same rosy complexions. There is roast beef in the Englishman just as there is rice in the Chinaman.

Indeed, how can one understand such people? How can you define people who make a point of never asking personal questions about their neighbors' private lives, but follow all the comings and goings and new acquisitions of their Queen as though they were the *concierges* of Buckingham Palace; who are stout champions of individual liberty, but close their pubs at three P.M. sharp; who don't like to talk, but adore orators; who hate heat, but love a good fire; who have an innate sense of grandeur, but who—from their cottages and ponies to their railway engines—carefully cultivate the small; who talk of trifles when sober and begin to talk of serious things when drinking; who do things like no one else in the world and yet are astonished that the rest of the world doesn't do the same; who consider *The Times* the most serious newspaper in the world, but reserve its front page for personal messages from gentlemen seeking traveling companions; who see their children caned by their masters without batting an eyelash, but cannot stand the sight of a crippled sparrow; who are suspicious of everything that isn't British, but who derive their national beverage from a Chinese-Indian shrub; who wouldn't dream of kissing in public in the subway or on the street, but who do it at Hyde Park or Maidenhead before a public that's twice as large; who abhor cross-breeding, but are themselves an extraordinary cross-mixture of Celts, Saxons, Scandinavians, and Normans; who reproach the French for living to eat, but spend their time nibbling odds and ends; who dress informally in their castles, but insist on donning gray bowler hats and carnations before going to feel the udder of a Yorkshire cow at an Olympia exhibition; who remain the cradle of the most unbending conservatism, but who served as the incubator for Karl Marx and Lenin; who enforce austerity on the Sabbath while distributing a Sunday scandal weekly to eight million readers; who manufacture *bidets* for the rest of the world, but won't have one in the house; who like to drive slowly while living, but get driven at breakneck speed in their Rollses when dead; who carry an umbrella when the sun is out and a raincoat when it pours; who are always chanting "Home, Sweet Home," but love to settle down abroad; who wouldn't for the world speak of the stomach, but who advertise contraceptives in their "chemist" shops; who are regarded as paragons of politeness, but who walk into restaurants ahead of their wives?

George Santayana
The Lion and the Unicorn c1916

EVERY ONE CAN SEE WHY the Lion should be a symbol for the British nation. This noble animal loves dignified repose. He haunts by preference solitary glades and pastoral landscapes. His movements are slow, he yawns a good deal; he has small squinting eyes high up in his head, a long displeased nose, and a prodigious maw. He apparently has some difficulty in making things out at a distance, as if he had forgotten his spectacles (for he is getting to be an elderly lion now), but he snaps at the flies when they bother him too much. On the whole, he is a tame lion; he has a cage called the Constitution, and a whole parliament of keepers with high wages and a cockney accent; and he submits to all the rules they make for him, growling only when he is short of raw beef. The younger members of the nobility and gentry may ride on his back, and he obligingly lets his tail hang out of the bars, so that the little Americans and the little Irishmen and the little Bolshevists, when they come to jeer at him, may twist it. Yet when the old fellow goes for a walk, how all the domestic and foreign poultry scamper! They know he can spring; his strength when aroused proves altogether surprising and unaccountable, he never seems to mind a blow, and his courage is terrible. The cattle, seeing there is no safety in flight, herd together when he appears on the horizon, and try to look unconscious; the hyenas go to snarl at a distance; the eagles and the serpents aver afterwards that they were asleep. Even the insects that buzz about his ears, and the very vermin in his skin, know him for the king of beasts.

But why should the other supporter of the British arms be the Unicorn? What are the mystic implications of having a single horn? This can hardly be the monster spoken of in Scripture, into the reason for whose existence, whether he be the rhinoceros of natural history or a slip of an inspired pen, it would be blasphemy to inquire. This Unicorn is a creature of mediaeval fancy, a horse rampant argent, only with something queer about his head, as if a croquet-stake had been driven into it, or he wore a very high and attenuated fool's cap. It would be far-fetched to see in this ornament any allusion to deceived husbands, as if in England the alleged injury never seemed worth two horns, or divorce and damages soon removed one of them. More plausible is the view that, as the Lion obviously expresses the British character, so the Unicorn somewhat more subtly expresses the British intellect. Whereas most truths have two faces, and at least half of any solid fact escapes any single view of it, the English mind is monocular; the odd and the singular have a special charm for it. This love of the particular and the original leads the Englishman far afield in the search for it; he collects curios, and taking all the nation together, there is perhaps nothing that some Englishman has not seen, thought, or known; but who sees things as a whole, or anything in its right place? He inevitably rides some hobby. He travels through the wide world with one eye shut, hops all over it on one leg, and plays all his scales with one finger. There is fervour, there is accuracy, there is kindness in his gaze, but there is no comprehension. He will defend the silliest opinion with a mint of learning, and espouse the worst of causes on the highest principles. It is notorious elsewhere that the world is round, that nature has bulk, and three if not four dimensions; it is a truism that things cannot be seen as a whole except in imagination. But imagination, if he has it, the Englishman is too scrupulous to trust; he observes the shapes and the colours of things intently, and behold, they are quite flat, and he challenges you to show why, when every visible part of everything is flat, anything should be supposed to be round. He is a keen reformer, and certainly the world would be much simpler, right opinion would be much righter and wrong opinion much wronger, if things had no third and no fourth dimension.

Ah, why did those early phrenologists, true and typical Englishmen as they were, denounce the innocent midwife who by a little timely pressure on the infant skull compressed, as they said, "the oval of genius into the flatness of boobyism"? Let us not be cowed by a malicious epithet. What some people choose to call boobyism and flatness may be the simplest, the most British, the most scientific philosophy. Your true booby may be only he who, having perforce but a flat view of a flat world, prates of genius and rotundity. Blessed are they whose eye is single. Only when very drunk do we acknowledge our double optics; when sober we endeavour to correct and ignore this visual duplicity and to see as respectably as if we had only one eye. The Unicorn might well say the same thing of two-horned beasts. Such double and crooked weapons are wasteful and absurd. You can use only one horn effectively even if you have two, but in a sidelong and cross-eyed fashion; else your prey simply nestles between, where eye cannot see it nor horn probe it. A single straight horn, on the contrary, is like a lancet; it pierces to the heart of the enemy by a sure frontal attack: nothing like it for pricking a bubble, or pointing to a fact and scathingly asking the Government if they are aware of it. In music likewise every pure melody passes from single note to note, as do the sweet songs of nature. Away with your demoniac orchestras, and your mad pianist, tossing his mane, and banging with his ten fingers and his two feet at once! As to walking on two feet, that also is mere wobbling and, as Schopenhauer observed, a fall perpetually arrested. It is an unstable compromise between going on all fours, if you want to be safe, and standing on one leg, like the exquisite flamingo, if you aspire to be graceful and spiritually sensitive. There is really no biped in nature except ridiculous man, as if the prancing Unicorn had succeeded in always being rampant; your feathered creatures are bipeds only on occasion and in their off moments; essentially they are winged beings, and their legs serve only to prop them when at rest, like the foot-piece of a motor-cycle which you let down when it stops.

The Lion is an actual beast, the Unicorn a chimera; and is not England in fact always buoyed up on one side by some chimera, as on the other by a sense for fact? Illusions are mighty, and must be reckoned with in this world; but it is not necessary to share them or even to understand them from within, because being illusions they do not prophesy the probable consequences of their existence; they are irrelevant in aspect to what they involve in effect. The dove of peace brings new wars, the religion of love instigates crusades and lights faggots, metaphysical idealism in practice is the worship of Mammon, government by the people establishes the boss, free trade creates monopolies, fondness smothers its pet, assurance precipitates disaster, fury ends in smoke and in shaking hands. The shaggy Lion is dimly aware of all this; he is ponderous and taciturn by an instinctive philosophy. Why should he be troubled about the dreams of the Unicorn, more than about those of the nightingale or the spider? He can roughly discount these creatures' habits, in so far as they touch him at all, without deciphering their fantastic minds. That makes the strength of England in the world, the leonine fortitude that helps her, through a thousand stupidities and blunders, always to pull through. But England is also, more than any other country, the land of poetry and of the inner man. Her sunlight and mists, her fields, cliffs, and moors are full of aerial enchantment; it is a land of tenderness and dreams. The whole nation hugs its hallowed shams; there is a real happiness, a sense of safety, in agreeing not to acknowledge the obvious; there is a universal conspiracy of respect for the non-existent. English religion, English philosophy, English law, English domesticity could not get on without this "tendency to feign." And see how admissible, how almost natural this chimera is. A milk-white pony, elegantly Arabian, with a mane like sea-foam, and a tail like a little silvery comet, sensitive nostrils, eyes alight with recognition, a steed such as Phoebus might well water at those springs that lie in the chalices of flowers, a symbol at once of impetuosity and obedience, a heraldic image for the daintiness of Ariel and the purity of Galahad. If somehow we suspect that the poetical creature is light-witted, the stern Lion opposite finds him nevertheless a sprightly and tender companion, as King Lear did his exquisite Fool. Such a Pegasus cannot be a normal horse; he was hatched in a cloud, and at his birth some inexorable ironic deity drove a croquet-stake into his pate, and set an attenuated crown, very like a fool's cap, between his startled ears.

Margaret Halsey
English Conversation 1938

THE BONELESS QUALITY of English conversation, so far as I have heard it, is all form and no content. Listening to Britons dining out is like watching people play first-class tennis with imaginary balls. No awkward pauses, no sense of strain, mar the gentle continuity of the talk. It goes on and on, effortlessly spinning words and words and yet more words out of the flimsiest material: gardening; English scenery; innocuous news items; yesterday's, today's and tomorrow's weather.

By the time this evening was over, I felt, intellectually, like a baby that is cutting its teeth and has nothing to bite on, but there are two things I like about this verbal thistledown. It is so skillful and practised, and also so remote and impersonal, that even I manage to hold my own in it—though ordinarily I am stiff-tongued to a degree which makes other guests think I must be one of the host's feeble-minded relatives and tactfully refrain from asking questions about me. Then, too, there is an aura of repose about this sort of conversation. These people do not talk, as so many Americans do, to make a good impression on themselves by making a good impression on somebody else. They have already made a good impression on themselves and talk simply because they think sound is more manageable than silence.

Ephraim Kishon
Two Sides of English Humour 1965

BESIDES THE ENDLESSLY RICH LANGUAGE, what this writer most envies his British fellow-humorist for is the extremely high guffawing-coefficient of British audiences. That is something bordering on the miraculous. Theirs is not simply a grateful public, but an attraction in its own right. I am mainly referring to the tornadoes of merriment at the popular radio shows of the BBC, which generally boil down to a repartee between two sleek-tongued comedians. We in Israel are privileged to hear them day after day, whenever we tune in to the British Army Broadcasting Station on nearby Cyprus.

The shortwave laugh-feast—there is no other way to describe it—starts out with a tremendous storm of applause, obviously a signal that the two protagonists have come onstage. Then one of them says in a broad cockney accent:

"What's eating you, Charlie?"

The audience reacts with thunderous laughter to this perfect take-off but the acclaim practically demolishes the radio set when the other fellow shoots back from the hip with:

"I've had a terrible headache since this morning."

The audience is shaking the rafters with their roars as the first one promptly tops this:

"And what makes your head ache, Charlie?"

At this point the guffaws become positively hysterical. An ecstatic spectator loses control over his senses and falls off his chair with a sharp report, while others struggle helplessly in the whirlpool of irresistible laughter. In the background one hears the sirens of approaching ambulances.

"Do I know?"

That's all they needed! The spontaneous gales of laughter turn into rhythmical handclapping of megaton intensity, with enthusiastic whistles renting the ether. A lady with a falsetto voice neighs like a horse, then goes out of her mind. The ushers remove her forcibly.

"Maybe you didn't sleep well last night, Charlie?"

Now that was rather weak. But never mind, you cannot score bulls' eyes all the time. Tension is fizzling out noticeably when Charlie saves the situation with a sensational improvisation:

"How could you sleep well with such a headache?"

At this point the last bastions of proverbial British reserve crumble in the earthquake-like roars of laughter. Only the prompt and effective intervention of the police flying squad prevents the situation from turning into utter chaos. Two fatalities.

Most of the tubes in the radio set have burned out. The Israeli listener sits bemused in front of his smoking radio, wondering what on earth had been going on there, in the London studio?

So, if for nothing else, just to solve the Cyprus riddle, it has been worth our while to come to England. Today we know: the two comedians are obviously wearing black bowler hats. * * *

The self-control and manners of the island dwellers never fail to amaze the foreign visitor. I shall never forget the day when, at a London railway station, a very fat man tried to board our chock-full train. He pushed and shoved, freely making use of his elbows, trying to make room for his great bulk and three suitcases. In our country, someone would long ago have knocked out some of his front teeth, but these well-mannered Englishmen were placidly watching the performance of this wild bull, their glances saying: "Such doings are below our dignity." At long last, an elderly gentleman remarked to our bullish friend:

"Why are you pushing, sir? Others, too, would like to sit."

"I don't care about others," he replied and went on bulldozing down the passengers. "Because of you, I'm not going to stand on my feet till Southampton."

No one argued with him, no one said another word. They ignored him and scornfully let him sit all the way. It is practically impossible to make an Englishman lose his temper. Especially since our train was going to Birmingham, a destination diametrically opposed to Southampton.

George W. Hills
The Noble Landlady 1914

THE GENUS ENGLISH LANDLADY may be of all styles, shapes, ages and sizes, but they all fly the same "social status" flag, married, widows and old maids alike, and the story of her life will be gratefully poured into your sympathetic ear if you betray the slightest willingness to listen. All of them tell it about the same way, with but little variation. English landladies are invariably descended from "gentry" and possess very wealthy relatives who live in luxury and exhibit a most cruel disregard of poor relations in the majority of instances, not even showing the faintest interest in your poor landlady's earthly existence. Forced therefore by a fate especially frosty to this particular guild, to acquire some sort of a genteel income, they advertise in the daily papers for "paying guests," which is polite English for "boarders" or "lodgers." The "paying guests" occupy the better portion of the premises, and the landlady's hitherto lonely or precarious existence as the decayed exponent of an alleged noble ancestry is thus rendered more or less commercially safe through the income paid her by the merry boarders. * * *

It would appear that the more "highly connected" these people are with mythical "genteel" ancestors, the further has been the fall and the longer their distance from home, so to speak. Apparently, when a member of the English gentry metamorphoses into a landlady they leave behind all that gentle womanly charm and grace which usually denotes high birth and education, acquiring instead a singular air of superiority over the common herd, and in some cases misplacing their h's and doing other curious things not at all characteristic of the nobility.

"May I enquire your name, madam," said I to my prospective landlady.

"My name is Mrs. 'awkins, sir."

"Mrs. 'enery 'awkins?" said I, jokingly.

"No sir—not 'enry, sir—Hedward."

"I feel so ignorant. I just wish I could tell if this is good or bad Constable country."

A MERRIE OLDE TOUR

&*Now it's time to take you for a ride ... I mean, to take a tour of Merrie Olde England. You've got to get out of the Big Prune and into the countryside. First, we'll tell you how to get around.*

Well, getting around England is not too exciting an experience. It's not too big; its trains run on time; its bus stops are clearly marked; its drivers are sane: even if they do drive on the wrong side of the road, at least they do it consistently. The English don't even mind a touch of fresh air in a bus or a train.

What you should get prepared for isn't putting up with English transportation, as you might elsewhere, but rather knowing the proper etiquette. The Mister Manners of Canada, Stephen Leacock, will prepare you for any eventuality. Then Mark Twain will tell of his rather subordinary experience on a train to London.

Stephen Leacock
Train Etiquette 1922

THE JOURNEY FROM LIVERPOOL TO LONDON, like all other English journeys, is short. This is due to the fact that England is a small country; it contains only fifty thousand square miles, whereas the United States, as every one knows, contains three and a half billion. I mentioned this fact to an English fellow-passenger on the train, together with a provisional estimate of the

American corn crop for 1922; but he only drew his rug about his knees, took a sip of brandy from his travelling flask, and sank into a state resembling death. I contented myself with jotting down an impression of incivility and paid no further attention to my fellow-traveller other than to read the labels on his luggage and to peruse the headings of his newspaper by peeping over his shoulder.

It was my first experience of travelling with a fellow-passenger in a compartment of an English train, and I admit now that I was as yet ignorant of the proper method of conduct. Later on I became fully conversant with the rules of travel as understood in England. I should have known, of course, that I must on no account speak to the man. But I should have let down the window a little bit in such a way as to make a strong draught on his ear. Had this failed to break down his reserve, I should have placed a heavy valise in the rack over his head so balanced that it might fall on him at any moment. Failing this, again, I could have blown rings of smoke at him or stepped on his feet under a pretence of looking out of the window. Under the English rule, as long as he bears this in silence you are not supposed to know him. In fact, he is not supposed to be there. You and he each presume the other to be a mere piece of empty space. But let him once be driven to say, "Oh, I beg your pardon, I wonder if you would mind my closing the window," and he is lost. After that you are entitled to tell him anything about the corn crop that you care to.

But in the present case I knew nothing of this, and after three hours of charming silence I found myself in London.

Mark Twain
The Scenery 1872

I T WAS MY PURPOSE TO SPY OUT THE LAND in a very private way, and complete my visit without making any acquaintances. I had never been in England, I was eager to see it, and I promised myself an interesting time. The interesting time began at once, in the London train from Liverpool. It lasted an hour—an hour of delight, rapture, ecstasy. These are the best words I can find, but they are not adequate, they are not strong enough to convey the feeling which this first vision of rural England brought to me. Then the interest changed and took another form: I began to wonder why the Englishman in the other end of the compartment never looked up from his book. It seemed to me that I had not before seen a man who could read a whole hour in a train and never once take his eyes off his book. I wondered what kind of a book it might be that could so absorb a person. Little by little my curiosity grew, until at last it divided my interest in the scenery; and then went on growing until it abolished it. I felt that I must satisfy this curiosity before I could get back to my scenery, so I loitered over to that man's end of the carriage and stole a furtive glance at the book; it was the English edition of my *Innocents Abroad!* Then I loitered back to my end of the compartment, nervous, uncomfortable, and sorry I had found out: for I remembered that up to this time I had never seen that absorbed reader smile. I could not look out at the scenery any more, I could not take my eyes from the reader and his book. I tried to get a sort of comfort out of the fact that he was evidently deeply interested in the book and manifestly never skipped a line, but the comfort was only moderate and was quite unsatisfying. I hoped he would smile once—only just once—and I kept on hoping and hoping, but it never happened. By and by I perceived that he was getting close to the end; then I was glad, for my misery would soon be over. The train made only one stop in its journey of five hours and twenty minutes; the stop was at Crewe. The gentleman finished the book just as we were slowing down for the stop. When the train came to a standstill he put the book in the rack and jumped out. I shall always remember what a wave of gratitude and happiness swept through me when he turned the last page of that book. I felt as a condemned man must feel who is pardoned upon the scaffold with the noose hanging over him. I said to myself that I would now resume the scenery and be twice as happy in it as I had been before. But this was premature, for as soon as the gentleman returned he reached into his hand-bag and got out the second volume! He and that volume constituted the only scenery that fell under my eyes during the rest of the journey. From Crewe to London he read in that same old absorbed way, but he never smiled. Neither did I.

The question in all of our minds (and if it isn't already, it will be now) is, why do the English drive on the left? For that matter, why do the English persist in saying such absurd things as "Cheerio!" and "old chap?" But this is not the section for that. And anyways, if we fill your mind too full of questions, you'll put this book down and start reading an encyclopedia from A to Z, which is not what we had hoped (we'd hoped you'd go out and buy another Humorists' Guide). So let's settle for why the English drive on the left, and let's leave the question to the masterful humorist H. Allen Smith.

H. Allen Smith
Why on the Left? 1952

THE NEXT TOPIC is one which I have been investigating at some length—why the English drive on the left-hand side of the road. There is only one place in the whole of England where it is legal to drive on the right (barring one-way streets) and that is the passage and court at the Strand entrance to the Savoy Hotel.

Before ever leaving New York I put the question to Mr. C. S. Forester. He said the custom was grounded in good sense and dated back to the period when many Londoners traveled to and fro on horseback. A horse, said Mr. Forester, is always mounted from the left side. It was a matter of convenience, then, that a man coming out of a shop or house or tavern would have his horse aimed toward the left, otherwise he'd have to walk into the mud and slop of the street to mount, and from this practice came the custom of bearing to the left in traffic. Sensible. Mr. Forester added that my forefathers, the founders of the American nation, reversed the custom after the Revolution out of sheer perversity.

On arriving in London I found another explanation in a guidebook. The author of this book said that the Pope and Napoleon were responsible. Some years before the reign of Bonaparte, the Pope came to visit Paris. Up to then there had been no rule about the movement of traffic. The authorities, however, decreed that Parisians should ride or drive on the right-hand side of the street, leaving the left-hand side clear for the movement of the papal carriage. Thus a custom was born and, when Bonaparte came along, he made it the law of the land. Moreover, as he conquered country after country, the right-hand rule was put in force in those lands until it became the general thing throughout continental Europe.

The British, however, hating Napoleon's guts, reversed the custom out of sheer perversity.

Now I had two conflicting theories and I told them to Nat Gubbins and he said they were both wrong. He said that Mr. Forester was correct in one detail—the custom really dated back to horseback riding. It came into being because men on horseback had a practice of running each other through with swords and since the right hand was usually the sword hand, Englishmen got into the habit of riding on the left-hand side of the road, the better to slash and thrust. Logical.

Here in the Garrick Club I now outlined these *three* theories and when I had finished, Mr. Barker smiled in his gentle way and said they were all wrong. The true answer, he said, was nautical. "All my life," he said, "I have understood that it is the custom to drive on the left because ships pass each other on the left. Given two ships approaching each other head on, it becomes necessary that a general regulation dictate the procedure. In such a contingency, the helmsman knows the rules—veer to the left and pass on the left, so, you see, our traffic moves actually by maritime law."

"Sounds sensible," I said. "Sounds logical. Are you sure of it?"

"I'm almost certain," he said. Then he glanced around the big room and said, "Ah!" He had spotted a retired Admiral and now both of us crossed the room to the Admiral's table, and Mr. Barker explained the question, citing his own theory on why English traffic moves to the left.

"Hadn't thought of it that way," said the Admiral, "but by jove I believe you're right. You've got a bit of something there."

He now drew a pencil from his pocket and quickly sketched the outlines of two ships approaching each other head on. He studied the sketch a moment. "No, by heaven!" he exclaimed. "You're wrong, man! In a situation such as this, the ships must show their red lights to each other—their port lights—which means they pass on the right. Frightfully sorry, old boy. My mistake. Must be some other explanation."

&Before we start traveling through the various regions of England, we'll start with three freewheeling architecturo-humorous tours, the first two of standing buildings by the big Mc's of modern American humor—Ruth McKenney and Phyllis McGinley—and then a look at ruins with American travel writer Charles S. Brooks.

Ruth McKenney & Richard Bransten
Pleasure Is Subjective 1950

NEVER SAW ANYTHING MORE GOTHIC than the Woolworth Building until I came to Europe; at which point I "did" (thoroughly) eleven large cathedrals in fourteen days. I can still remember dragging through St. Stephen's in Vienna, my feet on fire, my eyes bulging, and my whole soul protesting against even one more *small* flying buttress, to say nothing of a gargoyle. "Baroque," people said to me, "Middle Gothic, fenestration, Renaissance, Romanesque, spatial concepts, Ravenna influence, Greek revival, triforium, Palladian...."

"Ah, yes," I used to say, flashing my persecutors a Uriah Heep smile, "Middle Gothic? Of *course.*"

In the end I became rather dreamy; flying buttresses floated by overhead, gargoyles were wafted gently about in Byzantine spatial concepts, I could not remember why Baroque was supposed to be beautiful and, through it all, my feet hurt. Hideously. In conclusion, I am violently opposed to eleven cathedrals in fourteen days, and especially for the honest American tourist who did *not* grow up around the corner from either a Palladian façade or a triforium. Why on earth should it be assumed that a short sea voyage—Statue of Liberty to Southampton—makes a Middle Gothic fanatic out of somebody who has yet to see his first *Decorated* choir? Architecture requires time, and a good stout pair of walking shoes; then it can be delightful, the most exciting part of your English journey. But cathedrals, like drink, should be imbibed in moderation. Finally, no work of art can give pleasure without some discipline; Canterbury is sublime, but not to somebody wholly innocent of medieval philosophy. Architecture, like music, has its idiom; Mozart will be only sweet sounds without some grasp of musical form, and St. Paul's is just a forest of marble until you discover the Renaissance.

Which is not to say that you should spend your entire time in England holed up in your hotel room with the *Cambridge History of Architecture*. Be calm. After your first four Gothic cathedrals (providing you take them in slow, easy, thoughtful stages) you will recognize a *Perpendicular* window and a *Decorated* arch without severe mental strain; gradually, almost before you notice, you will develop taste and, above all, pleasure, in Architecture. Indeed, if you give yourself a chance, there is no reason why one of the most poignant experiences in your life should not be the lantern tower at Ely, or the choir at Canterbury, or the lovely little city of Bath.

Pleasure is subjective. Aesthetic experience can be described but not transmitted. There is no point in telling a tone-deaf listener that a Mozart sonata is beautiful; perhaps it is, but not for him. The same way with Durham Cathedral. Durham is an exquisite building—I think. So do a very large number of critics, poets, architects, and laymen. But you may feel no pleasure when you walk into Durham Cathedral, and it is pointless to insist that you *should;* joy cannot be compelled. Moreover, age and experience, knowledge and mood, and even feet, can affect aesthetic reactions; nobody ever can feel too great delight at Hampton Court with a large blister on his heel. There is no need to creep about in hangdog style if Westminster Abbey leaves you blank; aesthetic pleasure is like happiness—a by-product, an accident, a bonus.

Phyllis McGinley
A Tour of English Cathedrals
IN THE SUMMER (OR RAINY) SEASON c1955

WESTMINSTER ABBEY

I wandered lonely as a fareless cabby
Through miles and miles of the Royal Abbey,
Which some call stately and some call sinister
But most Americans call "Westminister,"
For I wanted to see, beneath the throne,
That Stone of Scone which is Scotland's Stone.

The Stone was the reason for my safari,
But, getting confused by the statuary,
By the granite poets and the marble dukes,
By generals and judges in carved perukes,
By king in his coffin, by knight in his stall,
I didn't see the Stone of Scone at all.

Though later, in a buttery, pondering alone,
I was served by the waitress with a scone of stone.

ST. PAUL'S

From the stone gallery there's a view
    Of London that is simply heaven.
To see it, all you have to do
    Is climb six hundred twenty-seven
Steps. It doesn't cost a penny.
The only thing is I found it exactly six hun-
    dred and twenty-six steps too many.

ELY

Although assembled of various famous styles,
And one of the vastest in all of the British Isles,
Ely, whenever it rains,
Makes one aware of the drains—
For the Master Builders, while certainly up and coming,
Didn't understand plumbing.

WELLS

All by themselves on the Bishop's Moat,
Two swans were somnolently afloat
Who didn't seem to care in particular
If naves were Gothic or Perpendicular,
Or faced with limestone or Purbeck marble,
But only that weather had stopped being horr'ble
And sun, for a moment, was edging through.
Then, prying a pebble out of my shoe,
I trudged off churchward to stare for a while
At the Tombs of the Saxons on the Northern Aisle.

NOTE ON THE PREVALENCE OF FEE-TAKING

I think in all of England's See
No verger dwells untipped by me.

SALISBURY

Salisbury had a splendid steeple,
    A cloister walk in good repair,
And lots of French and German people
    Reading their guidebooks everywhere.
Despite a rather ominous sky,
They all took pictures. So did I.

He loved the Chapter House; its gate
  Looked toward a river and a thicket.
Now, *was* it Salisbury where we ate
  A sole that wasn't quite the ticket,
Or farther on, at Bath? No matter—
It's where I found my Lowestoft platter.

NOTE ON THE PREVALENCE OF CHORISTERS

Nothing can glower
Like a tourist throng
Trapped for an hour
By Evensong.

SOME NOTES ON THE PREVALENCE OF
SEVENTEENTH-CENTURY CHURCHES

A couple of very industrious men
Were Grinling Gibbons and Christopher Wren.
Across the land,
While the nation gulped,
Christopher planned
And Grinling sculped,
Busy as bees in honeycombs.
Colonnades, porticoes, elegant domes,
Apses, transepts, naves, and chapels,
Pulpits and choirs with turned pineapples,
Pews of mahogany, ceilings of gilt—
Grinling carved as Christopher built,
All over England, an absolute host of them.
And I think by now I must have seen most of
    them.

CANTERBURY TALE

When April's dulcet showers begin,
Few rooms are free at the Falstaff Inn.
In May, in June, when bloom the roses,
The Abbot's Barton's guest list closes.
Comes on July, you'll find small bounty
Remaining at the cozy County.
But when sets in the August flurry,
Fly, Pilgrim, fly from Canterbury!

WINCHESTER

When we came into Winchester,
   Unsuppered and morose,
We saw a hundred swallows
   Fly circling in the Close.

Down the austere gray corridors
   No footsteps rang but ours,
And all the airs of evening
   Were spiced with gillyflowers.

Against the Canon's Garden
   A red-and-white marquee
Stood, gala, for tomorrow's
   Old Boys' and Parents' Tea,

And it had rained that morning,
   Would rain again that night,
But nothing then save silence
   Spoke in the colored light

Till a bird sang his Vespers
   From somewhere near at hand.
Then, suddenly, in focus
   We saw this Fortress stand,

This plot, this realm, this England,
    And truly wished it well
Before we sought in Winchester
    Our bleak two-star hotel.

Charles S. Brooks
A Weakness for Ruins 1924

WE CONFESS A WEAKNESS FOR RUINS. We may regret that Netley stands broken to the sky and our eye may grieve at columns whose purposes are shattered, but in our hearts we know that the remnant, like the leaves of Sibyl, is greater than the whole. For abbeys like Netley find their sharpest interest not so much in their beauty of line and decoration or even in the fashion with which nature reclaims their ruin, as in the spur they give our fancy to rebuild the life that once walked beneath their fallen vaults. Trim, perfect walls could hold us no such invitation to construct the past. It is a century that spoke with foreign thought, its strife headed to a different end and its piety does not trot with ours; yet here are the very stones worn in procession down to supper, here are the ovens that cooked a mightier race of beef, here are the gardens where crops were reaped, and walls that listened once to prayer and scandal, to sorrow and to laughter.

There is something of the curious housewife in all of us. We like to see how people really live and to observe the intimate contrivance of their daily habits. We peep about these ruins with a zest that we might apply to a neighbor's window. When God made the tree he contrived the knot hole for our gossip and satisfaction. There is a poem of Browning about a house with its front knocked off and its rooms bare against the street.

The owner? Oh, he had been crushed, no doubt!
"Odd tables and chairs for a man of wealth!
What a parcel of musty old books about!
He smoked—no wonder he lost his health!"

It piques our interest and if that house stood just around the corner the most incurious of us would pause a bit in passing. For myself, when lately a new subway in New York devastated a path among the crowded buildings of Greenwich Village, I frequently walked there to see how it cut its way through hall and bedroom. Suspended dizzily among the wreckage was a fragment of a parlor with scarcely its chairs removed, its wall paper still unfaded where a picture had been hung, a mantel where books and clock had stood. And this was but a life vilely in the present, without the softening glamor of long centuries to tint it with romantic color.

❧Our circuit of England will be a clockwise one, starting west from London. The first place the tourist heads for when he leaves London for the West is Oxford. I mean, the U.S. has its own university in its own Cambridge. Oxford is special. Rhodes Scholars go to Oxford. Oxford Movements come out. Everything about Oxford is ancient and lovely, except for the students, all of whom are young and some of whom are lovely. In some ways, Oxford embodies the traditions of England better than anything in London. And it's not just a tourist sight, except in the summer; it's a living, breathing place. It's like sneaking into the House of Lords.

Just to show how little things have changed, the advice given below by nineteenth-century travel writer Richard Harding Davis is good as new.

Richard Harding Davis
Oxford at Its Best 1894

THE TOWN OF OXFORD IS AT ITS BEST during the
week in which the eight-oared boats of the twenty
colleges belonging to the university row for mastery on
the river. It is then filled with people up from London.
The weather, which is always to be considered first, is
the best the year gives, the green quadrangles and the
flowers are more beautiful than at any other time, and
every afternoon the river overflows with boats. The
beauty of Oxford, as everybody knows, does not lie in
any one building or in any one street; it is the abundance
and continuing nature of its beauty which makes it what
it is. It is not like any other show town in that one does
not ride or walk from the inn to see a certain cathedral or
a particular monument. In Oxford with every step you
take you are encompassed and shut in with what is
oldest and best in architecture, with what is softest and
most beautiful in turf and in window gardens of flowers.
You cannot go to the corner to post a letter without
being halted by some iron gateway which you have not
seen before, or a row of mocking gargoyles, or a mysterious coat of arms, or a statue half eaten by the can-
nibals of Time and Weather. You rush through whole
streets—being in a hurry to see the boats start, or late for
a luncheon, or some such important matter—lined with
crumbling walls or marvellous façades, with glimpses
through great doorways of radiant gardens, or of oaken
halls hung with old paintings and marble tablets. They
are as much a matter of course as are the fire-escapes in
New York, and so common to the town that you see
them as a whole, and regard them as little as you regard
the signs on the houses as you rush past them on the
elevated. They form part of the very atmosphere, and

those who breathe this atmosphere for any length of time grow to consider Oxford as a home, and return to it after many years to find it just as dear to them and just as beautiful and almost as old. I think it is much better to take Oxford this way than to go over it piece by piece with Baedeker in hand to acquaint one's self with the window of the headless scholar, with the tower that Wolsey built overnight, and the room in which Dr. Johnson wrote something very important, the name of which I forget. Personally, I confess to not knowing the location of more than three of all the twenty colleges. They all seemed to me to run into one another. And then it really did not matter, for you were sure to reach the one for which you had started if you made a sufficient number of wrong turns, and asked your way from every third undergraduate, and disobeyed his directions implicitly. And then the Eights' week is not a time in which one can best linger before stained-glass windows. For the river calls you by day, and there are suppers at night, and the very much alive undergraduates are as worthy of consideration as those who have gone before, and who remain in memorial tablets or on darkened canvas.

Not far from Oxford is the lovely town of Salisbury, best known for its magnificent cathedral and its steak. Margaret Halsey takes a peak inside the cathedral (and later, in the TOURISTS section, English-American novelist W. H. Hudson looks at how we look at the cathedral). Anyone who goes to Salisbury can't help but go a few miles outside of town to where the stones known as Stonehenge stand. In the second selection, Charles S. Brooks points you elsewhere.

Margaret Halsey
A Bumper Crop of Dead Knights 1938

WE WALKED AROUND at a slow, ecclesiastical pace, while I looked about me and tried to feel equal to my surroundings. They were unbelievably pictorial—heavy trees and grey ranks of pointed arches; the lawn green in the sunlight with a full-blooded, lambent greenness such as I have never seen in America; the Cathedral tower holding itself up against the moving clouds; and the flower borders bravely being *gemütlich* in the teeth of all the ancestral grandeur. Some dozen or two choir boys in grey robes and white collars were scouring the plain with their Chaucerian draperies tucked into their pants pockets. Whether because it was Sunday or because they were under the influence of the churchly atmosphere, their noise sounded more temperate than boys' racket generally does. A portly old cleric in a wide-brimmed hat coasted out from behind a buttress, and the choristers magically coagulated into a double line and marched off, demure but glistening with perspiration.

Entering the Cathedral, I found myself confronted with two factors I had not counted upon. One was that for all the sunlit splendor of the exterior, the inside was morbidly, icily damp. The other was the unnerving discovery that if you tiptoe through a cathedral you feel sheepish and silly, but if you do not, you feel like a boor. However, there is a bumper crop of dead knights in Salisbury, and I enjoyed myself. Mine is not a tender nature, and ordinarily there is the same amount of sentiment in my disposition that there is in Caesar's *Commentaries,* but I have a sense of the past which could be laid out flat and made up into awnings. There is no stained, battered, worndown, gouged-out, hard-featured chair or table I will not have a fondness for, if I am assured it is an antiquity, and to stand on a piece of pavement which is being held up by the three remaining handfuls of Jane Austen or Edward the Confessor seems to me a breathtaking privilege. Then, too, it is fortifying to wander around among knights in effigy who look much the same, though they may have breathed their last two hundred years apart, or to examine recumbent stone bishops who have been giving up the ghost with pious regularity from the thirteenth century to the day before yesterday. It makes dying lose its customary aspect and begin to seem merely a slight but universal weakness, like catching cold.

Charles S. Brooks
Mightier Then Stonehenge 1928

EVERY TOURIST GOES TO STONEHENGE. It has won its place in school geographies and on steamship folders. Motorists mark it on their schedule. And Avebury is ignored. It is more remote, it is true—an extra map in the tonneau—and it stands neighbor to no cathedral city. But Avebury is mightier than Stonehenge—"a cathedral to a parish church"—older and of deeper historical suggestion. It is, furthermore, a pleasant village with two good inns; whereas Stonehenge stands barren on the plain.

It must be that tourists, when once their path is set, do not know how to change. Sheep have a hundred paths upon a hill, but Mr. Cook has one. Elephants marching tail in mouth to advertise a circus follow a route as predetermined. Savernake is lovelier than the New Forest, but it is not visited. Tamworth surpasses Kenilworth, but the crowd neglects it. Except for Sir Walter Scott, Kenilworth is dull, and there are a dozen castles that please the fancy more—Ragland, Harlech, Chepstow,

Carnarvon, Conway, in Wales alone, without mention of the Scottish border.

Stonehenge has profited doubtfully by its advertising, but Avebury may be seen in comfort without a shilling ticket or any char-à-banc rubbing against the ribs. There is a barbed wire fence around Stonehenge but, being as wire fences are, one can look through it. Nor have I ever discovered why tourists will pay money to go within a wire inclosure, when the stones are seen to better advantage from the road without a fee. But there are persons who must put their finger on any sacred thing.

Devonshire and Cornwall form a mysterious peninsula full of cliffs overlooking a rough sea that breaks against them, and vast moors that make one think of Thomas Hardy novels (though the Wessex of his novels is really Dorsetshire, the county at the base of the peninsula). Little is more romantic than this part of England, romantic in the English way of course, the basis for the gothic novels we New World types eat up. The West is also the land of King Arthur, the king we know and love better than any of the real kings of England. No one really knows where he might have lived, but every ruin seems to be the only possible place in which such a man could have been born. Charles S. Brooks will examine some of the candidates.

But first, with the help of English travel writer H. V. Morton, we will look at the place from which the New World began to be populated by the English: Plymouth, home of the Pilgrims, with and to whom we give thanks every year (which makes them the only people ever who can't say the world isn't grateful). Then travel writer Paul Theroux takes us to Newquay, further out and on the north shore of Cornwall, and shows us what a bed-and-breakfast resort is all about.

H. V. Morton
Mayflower House 1935

THE OLD SAILOR POINTED to the head of the jetty with his pipe.

"That it did, zur, in 1620, as you can see from that stone."

He got up and limped over to a stone set in the roadway.

"*Mayflower*, 1620," was the inscription.

"If you was an American you'd ask me to take your photograph on it," said the old man. "And quite right too. If it hadn't been for the *Mayflower*, where would America be now? Thank you, zur!"

He brightened considerably.

"See that house—No. 9, the Barbican—that's the house where the Pilgrim Fathers slept the night before they sailed."

"What? The whole hundred and twenty?"

"Well, zur, as many as could, maybe."

I went over to No. 9, the Barbican.

It may be one of England's undiscovered treasures. It is one of the few remaining Elizabethan houses on the Barbican. As one hundred and twenty Pilgrim Fathers had to find bed and breakfast as near the jetty as possible on September 5, 1620, it seems highly probable that some of them slept at No. 9. Anyhow it would not be difficult to make out an argument for it. The ground floor of the house is now a coal agent's office.

"I believe," said the man behind the counter, "that unless they can prove that the Pilgrim Fathers really did sleep here, this house may be pulled down in a slum improvement scheme."

It is surely the duty of Plymouth to solve this problem.

"It's strange that not many Americans know this house. It is not, I think, mentioned in the guide books. We call it 'Mayflower House,' and the tradition here on the Barbican is that the pilgrims put up here, and in other houses now pulled down, while their ships were overhauled."

I asked him if I might explore the old place.

"An old lady lives upstairs," he replied. "You might ask her."

I mounted a dark staircase. At the top, in a gloomy little room, an old woman was peeling potatoes. I told her I was interested in "the Mayflower." She dipped a potato in the water.

"I'm busy," she said.

I saw that quite a large pile of potatoes separated me from historical investigation.

"I can't show you over now," she said, "or what'll my men say if they find their dinners not ready?"

"Quite right," I said.

The work of the world must come first.

"You can take it from me," remarked the old woman, with an air of finality which no man would dare to question, "this is 'Mayflower House.' There's no doubt about it. I know it is."

"I begin to feel it is, too," I said.

"Do you?" she replied. "Well, if you come back some other day when I'm not busy maybe I'll take you over it; it's a rare queer old house."

She bathed another potato and assaulted it with a knife.

I went down the dark stairway into the Barbican....

A narrow flight of stone steps leads up to Plymouth Hoe. I mounted them. The sailing of the *Mayflower* was one of the most dramatic events of the last three hundred years. Think how much was storing up for the world when that little ship went Westward Ho!

As I stood overlooking the sea an unforgettable thing happened. The liner *Mauretania*, prompt to the minute, steamed slowly into the Sound and lay at anchor beyond the breakwater. Fussy little tenders steamed beneath her mountainous sides. There was great activity on her decks. The mails were lowered, the tender sped back with them towards Plymouth....

Slowly the long, slender ship moved out to sea again on her way to Southampton.

Could you round off a morning on the Barbican more perfectly?

Mayflower, 1620.

Mauretania, 1926.

When I reached the hotel I found it full of Pilgrim Fathers.

"Oh, say, get some ice water, and, waiter, three dry martinis. Gee lookit here! What's this chickfeed? Is this a sixpence?"

I had a swift vision of the first Pilgrim Fathers kneeling on the shores of Mass., returning thanks for their safe arrival. You know the picture? The wind blowing their hair; their broad felt hats in their hands; beyond, the inhospitable dunes so soon to blossom with safety razors and sock suspenders.

"Here's mud in your eye!" said one of the modern Pilgrims, tossing down his martini.

It is very rarely that life is so artistic.

Paul Theroux
At Home 1983

ABOUT A HALF-HOUR AFTER ARRIVING in New-quay I was sitting in a parlor, a dog chewing my shoe, and having a cup of tea with Florence Puttock ("I said leave that shoe alone!"), who was telling me about the operation on her knee. It was my mention of walking that brought up the subject of feet, legs, knees, and her operation. And the television was on—there was a kind of disrespect these days in not turning it on for Falklands news. And Queenie, the other Peke, had a tummy upset. And Mrs. Puttock's cousin Bill hadn't rung all day—he usually rang just after lunch. And Donald Puttock, who lisped and was sixty-one—he had taken early retirement because of his back—Donald was watching the moving arrows on the Falklands map and listening to Florence talking about ligaments, and he said, "I spent me 'ole life in 'ornchurch."

Somehow, I was home.

But it was not my home. I had burrowed easily into this cozy privacy, and I could leave any time I wished. I had made the choice, for the alternatives in most seaside towns were a hotel, or a guest house, or a bed-and-break-fast place. This last alternative always tempted me, but I had to feel strong to do it right. A bed-and-breakfast place was a bungalow, usually on a suburban street some distance from the Front and the Promenade and the hotels. It was impossible to enter such a house and not feel you were interrupting a domestic routine—something about Florence's sewing and Donald's absurd slippers. The house always smelled of cooking and disinfectant, but most of all it smelled of in-laws.

It was like every other bungalow on the street, except for one thing. This one had a sign in the window, saying VACANCIES. I had the impression that this was the only expense in starting such an establishment. You went over to Maynards and bought a VACANCIES sign, and then it was simply a matter of airing out the spare bedroom. Soon, an odd man would show up—knapsack, leather jacket, oily hiker's shoes—and spend an evening listening to the householders' stories of the high cost of living, or the greatness of Bing Crosby, or a particularly painful opera-tion. The English, the most obsessively secretive people in their day-to-day living, would admit you to the privacy of their homes, and sometimes even unburden them-selves, for just £5. "I've got an awful lot on my plate at the moment," Mrs. Spackle would say. "There's Bert's teeth, the Hoover's packed up, and my Enid thinks she's in a family way..." When it was late, and everyone else in bed, the woman you knew as Mrs. Garlick would pour you a schooner of cream sherry, say "Call me Ida," and begin to tell you about her amazing birthmark.

Bed and breakfast was always vaguely amateur, the woman of the house saying she did it because she liked to cook, and could use a little extra cash ("money for jam"), and she liked company, and their children were all grown up, and the house was rather empty and echoey. The whole enterprise of bed and breakfast was carried on by the woman, but done with a will, because she was actually getting paid for doing her normal household chores. No special arrangements were required. At its best it was like a perfect marriage; at its worst it was like a night with terrible in-laws. Usually I was treated with a mixture of shyness and suspicion; but that was traditional English hospitality—wary curiosity and frugal kindness.

The English required guests to be uncomplaining, and most of the lower-middle-class people who ran bed-and-breakfast places were intolerant of a guest's moaning, and they thought—with some justification—that they had in their lives suffered more than that guest. "During the war," they always began, and I knew I was about to lose the argument in the face of some evidence of terrible hardship. During the war, Donald Puttock was buzz-bombed by the Germans as he crouched under his small staircase in Hornchurch, and, as he often said, he was lucky to be alive.

I told him I was traveling around the coast.

"Just what we did!" Mr. Puttock said. He and Florence had driven from Kent to Cornwall in search of a good place to live. They had stopped in all the likely places. Newquay was the best. They would stay here until they died. If they moved at all (Florence wanted fewer bedrooms), it would be down the road.

"Course, the local people 'ere 'ate us," Mr. Puttock said, cheerfully.

"Donald got his nose bitten off the other day by a Cornishman," Mrs. Puttock said. "Still hasn't got over it."

"I don't give a monkey's," Mr. Puttock said.

Later, Mrs. Puttock said that she had always wanted to do bed and breakfast. She wasn't like some of them, she said, who made their guests leave the house after breakfast and stay away all day—some of these people you saw in the bus shelter, they weren't waiting for the number fifteen; they were bed-and-breakfast people, killing time. It was bed-and-breakfast etiquette to stay quietly out of the house all day, even if it was raining.

Mrs. Puttock gave me a card she had had printed. It listed the attractions of her house.

- TV Lounge
- Access to rooms at all times
- Interior-sprung mattresses
- Free parking space on premises
- Free shower available
- Separate tables

The lounge was the Puttocks' parlor, the parking space was their driveway, the shower was a shower, and the tables tables. This described their house, which was identical with every other bungalow in Newquay.

I was grateful for the bed-and-breakfast places. At ten-thirty, after the Falklands news (and now every night there was "Falklands Special"), while we were all a bit dazed by the violence and the speculation and Mr. Puttock was saying "The Falklands look like bloody Bodmin Moor, but I suppose we have to do something," Mrs. Puttock would say to me, "Care for a hot drink?" When she was in the kitchen making Ovaltine, Mr. Puttock and I were talking baloney about the state of the world. I was grateful, because to me this was virgin territory—a whole house open to my prying eyes: books, pictures, postcard messages, souvenirs, and opinions. I especially relished looking at family photographs. "That's us at the Fancy Dress Ball in Romford just after the war ... That's our cat, Monty ... That's me in a bathing costume..." My intentions were honorable but my instincts were nosy, and I went sniffing from bungalow to bungalow to discover how those people lived.

It was either that—the Puttocks in their bungalow—or the opposite—vast bare cliffs of windswept stone that were blasted by the Atlantic. I used to leave the bungalow and laugh out loud at the difference. The town of Newquay in its charmless way was bleaker than the cliffs. It was dreary buildings and no trees. But the visitors were decent folks, mainly old people who were rather overdressed for such an ordinary place. The men wore hats and ties and jackets, and the women dresses and pearls. It looked like churchgoing garb, but they were off to buy the *Express* or the *Telegraph* or to walk to the bandstand and back. They seldom strayed out of the town and were never on the cliffs.

In a month or so, Mr. Puttock said, it would all be roaring with yobboes—fat mustached youths and oafish girls, drinking themselves silly and doing damage, or at least leaving a trail of vomit along the Promenade. Mr. Puttock intimated that a population composed of the very old and the very young did not exactly make Newquay sparkle.

Charles S. Brooks
The Round Table 1924

SUSPENDED AT ONE END [of the great hall at Winchester] is a large wooden disk that is said to be King Arthur's round table. I take these legends with an easy credence and find myself at one with Thomas Fuller. Such tales, he wrote, are laid "at such a distance, they are cheaper credited than confuted." We are to run on these relics of King Arthur in several towns and districts. Winchester is but one of many towns which thinks it is Camelot; for it is a stupid tower of a stupid town, here in the west of England, that boasts of no lineage from these golden days. Nor can one quarrel with the repetition of a legend that sends through his memory the pleasant lines of Tennyson and Malory.

Yet Camelot, to satisfy the fancy, should be pitched more sharply on the hills. The walls should cling to the dizzy rock like the shining castle of a dream and its glittering spires should trip the running stars. It is my whim that sets Camelot on the Cornish coast beyond Tintagel where the rugged coast resists the ocean—man's last stronghold to the west. Here on a barren crag that is blinded by fog and wind a ruin of tumbled stones shows that once a building rose above the sea. Sheep nibble at the grass all day and rest in the hollows of the rock, but towers rise up at night and flourish in ancient magic till the dawn.

Be the truth what it may, it is a fine old table and if Arthur himself never tucked his silken legs beneath it, certainly it must have groaned for other and hungrier kings. The disk is marked from center to rim with bands of alternate color like a gambler's wheel. Is it possible that King Arthur set the table on a massive pin and spun it round? *Faites vos jeus, messieurs! Rien ne va plus!* If London could be coaxed here was a fortune surer than the tax of the Domesday Book.

May we suggest that our cherished primitives laid their shining fortune on the black and red—Launcelot and Elaine, Geraint and Enid, with their chips and noses on the cloth? Why is Malory silent of these diversions in gorgeous Camelot? Did the widow of careful Windsor lay a hush on Tennyson lest the fashion spread to soil the purity of Balmoral? I fancy John Brown in kilts as croupier. I would exchange a dozen jousts with knights in armor, the storming of a hundred castles, for a plain narrative of some such happy evening with its rattle of merry chips.

The custodian was concerned lest we doubt the authenticity of King Arthur's table; and finally we met him half way and agreed that if there had ever been a King Arthur and he had lived in Winchester and owned a table, it is likely that this was it.

What's north of London? Scotland, of course. Oh, yes, and all those cities that rock music comes from, like Liverpool and Manchester. No one goes there!

Well, there are a few places worth visiting. And when you consider, the fewer tourists, the nicer it is to go (unless there's a reason for them not to go; and there rarely is). There are places that are, in fact, heavily touristed: Cornedbeef-on-Rye or Calling-on-Avon or something of the sort, that place where Shakespeare is said to have lived, you know, that guy who is said to have written Shakespeare's plays, unless you prefer to think it was Francis Bacon-'n'-Eggs or some fellow from Middlesex, whichever one that might be. And then the Lake District to the West and York to the East. But I should let the humorists tell you: first, Margaret Halsey on Stratford-on-Avon; the great nineteenth-century American humorist, whose name is every bit as fun as his writing, Petroleum V. Nasby, on a young fellow's tour of the Midlands; American travel writer W. C. Falkner on sleeping in someone else's bed; and Mr. Scarlet Letter himself, Nathaniel Hawthorne, on a visit to Wordsworth's home in the Lake District.

Margaret Halsey
Poet Worship 1938

ANNE HATHAWAY'S COTTAGE and Mary Arden's cottage are sufficiently beautiful, with their brilliant gardens, to soften the most obdurate foe of quaintness. But like all the other high spots in Stratford, they have been provided with postcard stands and with neat custodians whose easy, mechanical Poet-worship had me looking sharply to see if they were plugged into the wall. All of Stratford, in fact, suggests powdered history—add hot water and stir and you have a delicious, nourishing Shakespeare. The inhabitants of the town occupy themselves with painting SWEET ARE THE USES OF ADVERSITY around the rims of moustache cups for the tourist trade; the wide, cement-paved main street is fringed with literary hot dog stands; and in the narrow lanes adjoining, wrinkled little beldames of Tudor houses wearily serve out their time as tea rooms.

It costs a shilling to cross any doorstep in Stratford, and once inside, the visitor finds himself on the very spot where Shakespeare signed his will or wrote *The Tempest* or did something or other which makes it necessary to charge an additional sixpence for the extra sanctity involved. Through all the shrines surge English and American tourists, either people who have read too much Shakespeare at the expense of good, healthy detective stories or people who have never read him at all and hope to get the same results by bumping their heads on low beams. Both categories try heroically to appear deeply moved, an effort which gives their faces a draped look. Were it not for the countryside round about, I would not stay an hour in Stratford—I keep expecting that somebody all dressed up as the immortal bard will come rushing out with a jingle of bells and a jovial shout, and I will

121

have to confess apologetically that I am a big girl now and too old to believe in Shakespeare.

Petroleum V. Nasby
A Midlands Diary 1882

ON OUR RETURN TO LONDON we met our old steamer friend Tibbitts's Lemuel, of Oshkosh. He had been traveling in the North of England, and tiring of the smaller cities and the country, had returned to London to "do it." He was rather puffy in the cheeks and rather bleary about the eyes, which showed a season of not altogether strict adherence to the precepts of Father Matthew. He was overjoyed at seeing us, as men always are at seeing anybody of whom they want something. He was in trouble.

"Look here," said Lemuel, "you are a good fellow, now, and I know you will help me out. You see I came over for improvement and experience, and to enlarge my mind, and all that sort of thing, and the old gentleman insisted that I should keep a diary, and note down *my* impressions of scenery, and industries, and modes of living, and all that, and send it to him regularly, and I must do it, or he will cut off the supplies, and bring me home."

"Well, that is easy enough. You have done it? You have kept a diary?"

"Yes, a sort of a diary. You see there were four of us in the party, devilish good fellows, one from Chicago, and two from New York, and we went to a lot of places, and saw a great deal, and I wrote in my memorandum book every day, but it was certainly the last thing I did before going to bed, about four o'clock in the morning, or a little later. What the old gentleman wanted was not only an account of all this rot, but *my* impression of the places, to develop me. You understand?"

"Yes; and a good idea it is. Did you write down your impressions of the places you visited?"

"Well, yes; but I am afraid they won't satisfy father. He is mighty particular, and awful sharp."

"Will you let me see your memorandum book?"

He handed it to me, and these are some of the entries, which were, no doubt, written at four in the morning, the last thing before getting into bed; and they were, unquestionably, his impressions. I select a few at random, these few being excellent samples of the whole lot:—

LEEDS—*Manufacturing city—Beer very bad—Scotch whisky tolerable, though I never liked it cold.*

BIRMINGHAM—*Manufacturing city—Beer bad—Not equal to our lager—No good beer in England— Stout rather better—Went in on stout.*

MANCHESTER—*Good bottle beer—Draft beer bad—All draft*—(this sentence was not finished, probably for reasons. He explained that that night he slept in his boots.)

SHEFFIELD—*Manufacturing city—found some genuine American bourbon, and went for it—it was refreshing, as a reminder of home—don't know about the beer—there's no place like home.*

NOTTINGHAM—*Don't know what the people do—a great many of them—Beer bad as usual— Guinness' stout in bottles fairish—Wish*—(another unfinished sentence, explained as before.)

And so on. I told Lemuel that it certainly would not do to send these impressions to his father, as evidently he observed only one side of English life; that he had taken his observations through a glass darkly, but that I really hadn't the time to write up a set for him, especially as I had not visited those places myself.

"But what am I to do?"

Advising him to procure a good guide-book, and remain sober for a week, and get to work, we parted.

W. C. Falkner
Sir Walter Scott Slept Here 1884

KENILWORTH, JUNE 18, 1883. I have somehow managed to get myself considerably mixed with the name and writings of Sir Walter Scott. I rose fifty per cent in my own estimation this morning when I was informed by the landlord that I had slept in the identical room occupied by the famous novelist and poet.

"Why, sir, it is a fact," said my host, "that Sir Walter wrote *Kenilworth* in that very chamber. He slept in the same bed you reposed on last night."

"Have the sheets been changed since he slept there?"

The answer to this question was too much tinctured with irreverence to look well in print.

"Did Sir Walter leave any message or papers here for me?" I meekly inquired.

"What in the deuce did Sir Walter Scott know or care about you?"

"That is the very thing I am trying to find out. He certainly did not know I was coming here to compose poetry in his room, else he would have left some suggestions or advice for me."

More irreverence from the host as he rapidly walked away.

"This landlord thinks there is something wrong with your mind," said the courier.

"That proves his good sense," I replied. "I have arrived at a conclusion of that sort myself."

Nathaniel Hawthorne
Tender Recollections 1855

WE OUGHT TO HAVE BEEN SEEN De Quincey's former residence and Hartley Coleridge's cottage, I believe, on our way, but were not aware of it at the time. Near the lake there is a stone-quarry, and a cavern of some extent, artificially formed, probably by taking out the stone. Above the shore of the lake, not a great way from Wordsworth's residence, there is a flight of steps hewn in a rock and ascending to a rock seat where a good view of the lake may be attained; and, as Wordsworth has doubtless sat there hundreds of times, so did we ascend and sit down, and look at the hills and at the flags on the lake's shore.

Reaching the house that had been pointed out to us as Wordsworth's residence, we began to peer about at its front and gables, and over the garden wall, on both sides of the road, quickening our enthusiasm as much as we could, and meditating to pilfer some flower or ivy-leaf from the house or its vicinity, to be kept as sacred memorials. At this juncture a man approached, who announced himself as the gardener of the place, and said, too, that this was not Wordsworth's house at all, but the residence of Mr. Ball, a Quaker gentleman; but that his ground adjoined Wordsworth's, and that he had liberty to take visitors through the latter. How absurd it would have been if we had carried away ivy-leaves and tender recollections from this domicile of a respectable Quaker! * * *

In front of the house there is a circular terrace of two ascents, in raising which Wordsworth had himself performed much of the labor; and here there are seats, from which we obtained a fine view down the valley of the Rothay, with Windermere in the distance—a view of several miles, and which we did not suppose could be seen, after winding among the hills so far from the lake. It is very beautiful and picture-like. While we sat here, S— happened to refer to the ballad of little Barbara Lewthwaite, and J— began to repeat the poem concerning her, and the gardener said that "little Barbara" had died not a great while ago, an elderly woman, leaving grown-up children behind her. Her marriage-name was Thompson, and the gardener believed there was nothing remarkable in her character.

Apart from Canterbury, the eastern and southeastern parts of England are probably the areas foreign visitors head for the least (the English flock to them themselves; please note the relationship). Therefore, we have only one selection on that part of the world, a look at one of the most exciting of English resorts, Margate, by Margaret Halsey.

Margaret Halsey
The Pagan Abandon of Margate 1938

THE WALK TO MARGATE was along chalk cliffs above the sea, but it led into an increasingly thicker miasma of those Greco-like buildings the late Victorians were fond of putting up at summer resorts. Margate, they say, has the finest air in England. In reality, it has the only air in England. The rest of the country has to get along the best it can with an alien compound which shuffles into the nostrils like disinherited soup.

The English always speak of Margate as a place of vulgar and feverish gaiety, but the beach and promenade, at least, look to an American like a Quaker meeting. The sun is weak and the English are modest, so there is hardly any more flesh on view than there is in Piccadilly Circus. The bathers do not run races or play ball or stand on their hands or carry on conversations with friends a quarter of a mile away. Instead, they knit or hold hands or merely sit and stare out to sea. On the promenade grass, a few solemn individuals throw cricket balls with an overhand gesture which reminds the startled foreigner of a ten-year-old girl resigning from the neighborhood baseball team in a towering huff. The pagan abandon of Margate could be scraped together and piled up under a thimble, but the visitors look as if it would be a positive pleasure to go home on a crowded subway with them at the end of the day.

Of course, you won't be able to visit half these places or do half the things the authors have done. In fact, you might not be able to go to England at all. Zillions of wonderful events will be going on this year, not to mention billions of sales and millions of exhibitions, and you'll be missing them all. But not to worry; American humorist extraordinaire Robert Benchley will put your feelings to rest.

Robert Benchley
What We Missed 1932

HERE IT IS AUTUMN AGAIN, and a great many of us didn't get to Europe—again. What with one thing and another (both really the same thing in banking circles) we decided that it would be more fun this year just to stick around home. One can always dash off on little week-end trips and get just as dusty and grimy and lose just as much luggage as on a whole European tour. And it really doesn't cost so very much more money to stay at home than it does to travel abroad.

However, it looks as if we really had missed something this year by spending the season in the United States.

According to that little schedule which is sent out every year telling what is going on in the British Isles, we missed some perfectly corking sporting events in England. If I were quite sure how it is done, I would kick myself for having let the chance go by.

According to my schedule (this is as of 1932, mind you, so don't try to go by it for next year), on May eighth there was the "Furry Dance" at Helston in Cornwall; on May fourteenth the "Ceremony of Well-dressing" at Tissington in Derbyshire; on May twenty-fifth the "Ceremony of Dunmow Flitch" at Little Dunmow, Essex; on August eighth "Rush-Bearing" was revived at Grasmere in the Lake District; and on September seventh the "Dance of the Deer Men" came off at Abbots in Staffordshire. All of these come under the head of "Old Customs," so I gather that the people concerned know what to do when the time comes.

I think that most of all I should have liked to see the "Ceremony of Dunmow Flitch" at Little Dunmow. I don't imagine that bad weather would interfere very much with flitching, for it sounds like something that you could do just as well indoors as out in the open. I suppose that, for weeks ahead of the celebration, the young men of Little Dunmow train and diet and practice in order to be in perfect condition for May twenty-fifth.

"It's no good asking Georgie to the party," they probably say. "He's saving himself for the Flitch next week."

And when the Big Day arrives, and the flitchers are all assembled in their gay costumes (I have a feeling that a flitching costume cannot be worn for anything else but flitching and is put away in the attic directly the ceremony is over) the excitement in Little Dunmow passes belief, and the chorus of "Gorms" and "Oooms!" which shake the walls of the old town probably make our cheering sections sound like classes of deaf mutes. (I know that they don't say "Gorm" and "Ooom" in Essex so much, but there is nothing to prevent them from importing a gorm-ing and oooming section from Yorkshire in case they want to have things correct for the occasion.)

The "Furry Dance" in Cornwall has, as its main feature, a maneuver which might, and then again might not, be agreeable. In the "Furry Dance" all the inhabitants of Helston dance right through each house in town, in the front door and out the back, until they have been the rounds. Now this might be all very well for the dancers, provided each house *has* a back door, but I can imagine some unfortunate citizen who, having spent the evening before in the tap-room getting primed for the event, might possibly not be so crazy about having the entire township dancing through his bedroom in the morning. I should think that to wake up with a hangover, in a condition where every consideration and tenderness should be shown, and just as you were wondering which head to put on, to have the front door flung open and a line of cheering, merry-making dancers come tripping through, around the chairs, over the sofas, huzza-huzzoo, and out the back door, would be just a little more than one sick man could stand. And I'll bet they don't stop at just dancing through the house, either. There are probably bucolic wisecracks and a great deal of "Get up, get up, you lazyhead!" as they skip around. One person alone coming in, all fresh and brisk, would be too many under the circumstances. To have the whole township prancing through must be pretty discouraging. The wonder is that there are any people left in Helston at all.

Although I am sorry to have missed the National Carnation Show in London on July fourteenth, I have already got my disappointment under control. The carnation, or "pink," has really very little to recommend it as a source of excitement. Carnations and a species of dessert called "junket" always seemed to me to be in the same class spiritually, and although the young bloods have taken to wearing them (carnations, not junket) in their lapels with evening clothes, they still remain pretty fairly limited in their appeal to the senses. I hope that the Carnation Show was not held in a large hall, for it must have been difficult to think up combinations of carnations which would impel the visitor to go on from exhibit to exhibit. Aside from a display of the conventional red, pink, and white (with possibly those which are dyed green for St. Patrick's Day) there doesn't seem to be much that can be done with carnations except to bank them together in floral pieces with "Dear Bill" or "Success" picked out in red letters. They also make up into a tasty "Gates Ajar." But a whole horticultural hall full of them might pall a little, unless the visitor had been drinking before he came. On the whole, I am least sorry to have missed the National Carnation Show of all the treats offered by Great Britain during the summer.

August was a big month in British sports, with "Shakespeare Week for Overseas Bowlers" from the first to the fifth at Stratford-on-Avon and the rowing race "for Doggett's Coat and Badge" on the second. The English Folk Dance Society also had a meeting at Malvern during the first two weeks of the month. Whatever the English Folk Dance Society worked up during their festivities we shall probably get over here in America in some form or other during the coming year, so it doesn't make much difference having been absent from that. (And it won't make any difference if we are absent from the demonstrations when they are brought over here, either.)

The race for "Doggett's Coat and Badge" was probably just a boat race which, unless the speaker of the day got nervous and called the prize "Badgett's Cat and Dog" (which is unlikely), would offer no more startling features than a regular boat race—or, in other words, no startling features at all.

But in the "Shakespeare Week for Overseas Bowlers" there is a certain element of mystery. A "Shakespeare Week" would be understandable (though not to be recommended) and overseas bowlers are probably very nice people who bowl well, otherwise they wouldn't have taken the trouble to come across the ocean to do it. But where is the tie-up between Shakespeare and bowlers? I haven't gone through my Shakespeare much lately, and I certainly don't intend to for the purposes of this summary. But, as I run his plays and sonnets over in my mind, I can remember nothing which would have made him the patron saint of bowling, or would have endeared him to bowlers, especially overseas bowlers. The local bowling club at Stratford-on-Avon might well be called the Shakespeare Social and Nine-Pin Club, just as there might be a Henry Wadsworth Longfellow Skating Rink in Cambridge or a Betsy Ross Pimiento-and-Cream-Cheese Sandwich in Philadelphia. But, for overseas bowlers to make a pilgrimage to the shrine of the Bard of Avon can be explained only by the possibility of their having seen pictures of the beard and neck-ruffle and mistaking Sir Francis Drake for Shakespeare, a confusion that could so easily happen.

And so we see, that by sticking around home last summer, we missed a whole series of exciting events which, by sticking around home next summer, we may be able to miss again.

"Qu'est-ce que c'est, ce'toad-in-the-hole'?"

Osbert Lancaster

❧Amusements

❧Well, in the LONDON AMUSEMENTS *section, we followed the wise rule that if you can't say anything nice, don't say anything, and so said nothing about English food. Furthermore, English food is not really an amusement, but that's splitting hairs, isn't it, which is an activity comparable to eating fish in newsprint or steak & kidney pie. Well, now we feel more foolish and so, to accompany the amusing illustration on the opposite page, we will give Ruth McKenney & Richard Bransten as well as Karel Capek a chance to say at least a couple of words about English tourist cuisine.*

Ruth McKenney & Richard Bransten
Simply Frightful 1950

ON THE LUNCH SITUATION: Windsor is a tourist town. English food is seldom *very* good; but under the stress and strain of grand-scale *tourisme*, the English simply lose their grip and go all to pieces. It is odd. The French have the theory that history takes a lot out of the traveler and also that tourists are apt to remember what they eat in scenic locations. Across the Channel, there is a good deal of putting the best foot forward at Versailles cafés; and restaurants in Chartres are so good that *some* tourists go all the way from Paris just to gallop through the Cathedral at a brisk trot *(pour gagner un bon appétit)* after which they retire to a five-course luncheon, red and white wine, champagne with the fruit. But at Windsor the emphasis is on high thinking and plain—even atrocious—living. The Castle is wonderful, but the restaurants feature cabbage bathed in Ye Olde Englyshe hot water, and rare Tudor trifle with plenty of lukewarm custard sauce. As a generalization, Windsor eating establishments are awful beyond belief, and only rivaled by their opposite numbers in Stratford and Warwick. I have heard sharp disputes break out, among American tourists, on the relative horrors of eating at Warwick or at Windsor, but I feel little good can come of these distinctions. Let us face it: tourist food in England (a separate category from ordinary, usual English food) is vengefully—and stupidly—frightful, and has to be met at first hand to experience the full revulsion. The last time I lunched at Warwick, I heard a Belgian at the next table ask the waitress, *"Tiens, mademoiselle, qu'est-ce que c'est ce toad-in-the-hole?"*

"Ha," I said strictly to myself, "he'll find out."

He did, too.

"Horreur!" he kept shouting, but nobody paid any attention. You are not *expected* to like what you eat at English tourist resorts; the theory is, the traveler has lunch to keep up his strength, and no consideration is given to his pleasure, comfort, health or morale when he takes his midday repast.

With all this as a preface, I will cautiously—very cautiously—remark that when Richard and I go to Windsor (which in the summer is fairly often, in the company of visiting American cousins) we book a table in advance at the hotel which has a pleasant terrace overlooking the river. This hostelry is charmingly situated, as they say, and sometimes puts duck on the menu; their afternoon teas are also quite good.

But if the tables are all taken at the hotel, resign yourself to the standard Windsor—English tourist—cuisine; after all, you have not lived fully until you have eaten trifle (with custard sauce) under William the Conqueror's frowning battlements. Much later, it will seem funny.

Karel Capek
Hard Knox 1925

THERE ARE TWO KINDS of English cooking: good and average. Good English cooking is simply French cooking; average cooking in an average hotel for the average Englishman explains to a large extent the Englishman's bleakness and taciturnity. Nobody can beam and warble while chewing pressed beef smeared with diabolical mustard. Nobody can exult aloud while ungluing from his teeth quivering tapioca pudding. A man becomes terribly serious if he's given salmon daubed with pink dextrin. And if for breakfast, lunch, and dinner he has something which, when alive, was a fish, and in the melancholy condition of edibility is called fried sole; if three times a day he soaks his stomach with a black brew of tea; and if he drinks his fill of bleak light beer; if he partakes of universal sauces, preserved vegetables, custard, and mutton—well, he has perhaps exhausted all the bodily enjoyments of the average Englishman and he begins to comprehend his reticence, solemnity, and austere morals. On the other hand, toast, baked cheese, and fried bacon are certainly the heritage of Merry Old England. I'm convinced that old Shakespeare did not soak himself with tannin; and old Dickens, as long as he lived, did not once make merry on preserved beef; as for old John Knox, I'm not so sure...

Now that you've digested that, we will turn to one of the most memorable experiences we take back with us from traveling in England: the visit to the truly English pub. Even if we wouldn't be caught dead in a neighborhood bar back home, we can't help but be drawn to the pub. Their names are so charming; their reputations so atmospheric; and they're everywhere, the further from civilization the better. Anglo-American storyteller Eric Knight, best known as the author of Lassie Come Home, *takes his Californian protagonist, and us, into a Yorkshire pub and watches with amusement as the two civilizations—and languages—meet head-on.*

Eric Knight
All Yankees Are Liars 1938

> *You can always tell the Irish,*
> *You can always tell the Dutch.*
> *You can always tell a Yankee;*
> *But you cannot tell him much.*

MR. SMITH WAS PLEASED with The Spread Eagle. He was pleased with Polkingthorpe Brig. The village was off the beaten track—the truly rural sort of English village the American always wants to see.

The inn was low and rambling, with great sloping roofs. Over the door swung the sign—a darksome bird in a weather-beaten setting.

Everything justified his decision to take this bicycle trip up into the north—the mullioned windows, the roaring fire, the Yorkshire accents of the men who shuffled over the sanded stone floor of the low-ceilinged room as they played darts. Mr. Smith was almost beginning to understand what they were talking about. During his excellent high tea he had sorted out the four men playing darts.

One was Saw Cooper, a farmer; a small old man was referred to as Sam; a young, bright-faced lad who played darts left-handed was Gollicker Pearson; and the fourth, a huge man, was just called Ian.

Mr. Smith watched them play, listening to the endless thwock of the darts in the cork board as he finished his meal. The barmaid, plump, corn-haired, came toward him, her apron rustling stiffly.

"Would there be owt else?"

"No. It was a very good meal." Mr. Smith smiled. He wanted to make the girl talk some more. "Er—what do they do for fun in this place of an evening?"

"Foon?" she repeated. "Well, they sit here—or o' Satday neights lots o' fowk goa ovver to Wuxley to t'pictures." She waited. "They gate Boock D'Arcy i' T' Singing Cowboy," she added suggestively.

Mr. Smith had already become acquainted with British cinemas in small towns. Also, he was a Southern Californian, and had that familiarity with movies that belongs to all Southern Californians. He had no inclination to go four miles to see a last year's Class B Western. "No. I think I'll have another ale and sit here," he said.

"If tha'll sit ovver by t'fire, Ah'll bring it to thee theer. Than Ah can clean oop here."

Mr. Smith sat on the bench by the generous fire and nursed his ale. The dart game came to an end with Saw Cooper losing and paying for the round. The men brought their mugs to the fire. Mr. Smith shifted politely. The men, in the presence of a stranger, grew quiet. Mr. Smith decided to put them at ease.

"Pretty chilly for an October evening, isn't it?"

The men considered the remark, as if looking at both sides of it. Finally Saw Cooper spoke.

"Aye," he said.

The others nodded. There was silence, and the five regarded the fire. Then, suddenly, young Gollicker smiled.

"Tha shouldn't heed t' cowd, being a Yankee," he said.

"Ah, but I'm not a Yankee," Mr. Smith said.

They stared at him in disbelief.

"Yankees," he said, "come fro' t' United States."

"Well, yes. New England is a part of the United States," Mr. Smith said. "But it's thousands of miles away from where I live. In fact, believe it or not, I should think you're closer to the Yankees than I am. You see, the United States is a big country. In the part where the Yankees come from, it gets very cold in the winter. Where I am—in Southern California—it never snows. Why, I've never known it to snow there in all my life."

"No snow?" Gollicker breathed.

Mr. Smith smiled. For, after all, he was a Southern Californian—and they were discussing climate. "No snow," he said. "In wintertime we have a bit of a rainy season, but after February it clears, and then it doesn't even rain for nine months—not a drop."

"Noa rain for a nine month—noan at all?" Saw Cooper asked.

"Not a drop. Day after day, the sun comes out, clear skies, never a drop of rain for nine months. Never!"

"Whet do ye graw theer, lad?" Saw asked, slyly.

"Lots of things. Truck, vegetables, oranges—all kinds of things."

There was a silence again. Big Ian took a breath.

"Orinjis," he said, and then took another breath, "graw i' Spain."

He looked at Mr. Smith so emphatically that Mr. Smith nodded. "Oh, yes," he said. "They grow in Spain, too, I understand."

"Orinjis," Ian repeated, "graw i' Spain."

That seemed to settle the question. They all looked in the fire in silence. Saw Cooper sniffed.

"Whet else graws theer?"

"Well, I have a ranch there; we grow alfalfa."

"Whet's that off to be?"

138

"Alfalfa? We use it for hay. It's a desert plant originally, but it thrives in California. We get eight cuttings a year."

"Eight cuttings o' hay a year?"

"Eight cuttings a year."

The little man, Sam, spoke for the first time: "Mister, if it doan't rain for a nine month, how can ye get eight cuttings o' hay a year?"

"Oh, that's easy," Mr. Smith said. "We irrigate the land." He went into a short but conclusive description of irrigating.

"Heh," Saw Cooper said. "Wheer's this heer water come from?"

"In the San Fernando Valley we buy it from the water company."

"Wheer do they get it?"

"From reservoirs."

"If it doan't rain, where's t' reservoys get t' watter?"

"Oh, we pipe it down from five hundred miles north. It rains a lot up there."

"And ye sprinkle t' farming land out o' t' watter tap. How mony acres hesta?"

"It isn't like sprinkling from the tap, of course. I used that to illustrate. The pipes are large—we have fourteen-inch valves on our pipes. We flood the land—cover it right over with water."

Saw looked in the fire. "Does corn graw theer?"

"Well, generally our land is too valuable to put into corn. But it will grow corn fourteen feet high."

They made noises in their throats and shifted their feet.

"Fohteen foot," Saw breathed. "Eigh, ba gum!"

"Mister," Sam said, "Once Ah were oop to see t' Firth o' Forth brig. Ah suppose they hev bigger brigs i' Yankeeland?"

Mr. Smith should have touched on the new Oakland bridge, but then, he was a *Southern* Californian.

"We have bridges, but they're building tunnels under the rivers now."

139

"Whet for?"

"Well, there's so much motor traffic."

"How mony moatorcars goa through 'em?"

Mr. Smith lit his pipe happily. They seemed quite interested in America.

"I couldn't say. The way they turn 'em out, I should say there's hundreds of thousands."

"How fast do they turn 'em out?" Gollicker asked.

"I don't know. I know they roll out finished at the rate of one every couple of minutes."

"And they goa i' tunnels, not i' brigs?" Sam commented.

"Oh, we have some bridges."

"Big uns, Ah suppose."

"Well," Mr. Smith said modestly, thinking of the Pulaski Skyway coming into New York, "we have some that go right over entire towns. You're practically on one bridge for miles."

Saw Cooper spat in the fire. "How mony fowk is there in all America?"

Mr. Smith didn't know, but he felt expansive. And after all, there was South America too.

"A quarter of a billion, I should say," he hazarded.

"A quarter of a billion," they repeated. Then they stared at Mr. Smith, and he became aware of their disbelief.

"Wait a moment," he said. "I think a billion is different in America from here. It's a thousand million in America and a million million here, isn't it?"

"A billion," said Ian slowly, "is a billion."

The others nodded, and then Ian stood. The others rose too.

"Oh—er—wait a minute. Won't you all have a drink with me?" Mr. Smith invited.

"Us is off to play darts for a round—us four," Ian said, meaningly.

The other three laughed.

140

"Ah knew them theer brigs o' thine'd hev to be big," Saw Cooper said as a parting shot as he swung over the bench. "That's so's they'd be able to goa ovver wheat what graws fohteen foot high when ye sprinkle it fro' t' watter tap."

He grinned at the others in victory.

"I didn't say wheat; I said corn," Mr. Smith protested.

"Same thing," Saw snapped.

"It isn't. Wheat grows in an ear. Corn grows on a cob; it has broad long leaves."

"Heh! That's maize," Saw said.

Big Ian stepped between Saw Cooper and Mr. Smith.

"Now, lad," he said flatly, "tha said corn, and Ah heeard thee. Thee and thy orinjis, and farming out o' t' watter tap, and brigs ovver cities, and it nivver rains, and denying th' art a Yankee, and a billion is a billion and yet it ain't. Tha't tripped thysen oop a dozen times, it seems to me. Now, hesta owt to say?"

Mr. Smith looked at Big Ian, standing belligerently with legs widespread and his thumbs in the waistband of his corduroy trousers. He looked round and saw everyone in the inn waiting, silent.

Then a curious thing happened. In that minute the smell of soft-coal smoke and pig-twist tobacco and ale was gone, and instead Mr. Smith was smelling the mixed odor of sun-baked land and citrus blossom and jasmine and eucalyptus trees, just as you smell it in the cool darkness coming across the San Fernando Valley. And he was homesick. Suddenly it felt unreal that he should be so far from home, sitting in an English inn with these men about him. He looked up at the faces, forbidding in their expression of disapproval. And he began to laugh.

It was all so unreal that he laughed until he cried. Every time he looked up he saw the faces, now even more comical in their bewilderment than they had been in their disapproval. They stared at him, and then Big Ian began to laugh.

"Eigh, Ah'll be jiggered!" he roared. "Drat ma buttons if Ah won't!"

It was Mr. Smith's turn to be puzzled now.

Big Ian roared, and suddenly slapped Mr. Smith on the back so heartily that his chin flew up in the air and then banged back on his chest. The others looked on in amazement.

"Why, whet's oop, Ian?" Saw asked.

"Why, ye gowks!" Ian roared. "He's laughing at ye! He's been heving us on! Sitting theer for an hour, keeping his mug straight and telling us the tale! And us swallering it, thinking he was serious!"

"But," Mr. Smith said— "but you don't—"

"Nay, now no moar on it!" Ian roared. "Ye've codded us for fair, and done it champion! Lewk at owd Sam's face!"

The others regarded Ian and scratched their heads and grinned sheepishly, and finally looked at Mr. Smith in admiration.

"But—" Mr. Smith began again.

"Nay, now, ye copped us napping," Ian said, "and here's ma hand on it. Soa we'll hev noa moar—onless ye'd like to tell us whet Yankeeland's rightly like."

Mr. Smith drew a deep breath. "Well, what would you like to hear about?"

"About cowboys," young Gollicker breathed. "Werta ivver a cowboy?"

For a moment Mr. Smith stood on a brink, and then an imp pushed him over.

"Of course I've been a cowboy—naturally," Mr. Smith said. "What would you like to hear about it?"

"Wait a minute," Gollicker said. They all adjusted themselves on the bench. "Now," he went on, "tell us about a roundup—tha knaws, 'Ah'm heading for t' last roundup,' like Bing Crosby sings."

Mr. Smith held his mental breath and plunged.

142

"Ah," he said. "A roundup and the life of a cowboy. Up at the crack of dawn, mates, and down to the corral. There you rope your horse—"

"A mustang?" Gollicker asked.

"A mustang," Mr. Smith agreed.

"A wild one off'n the prairies, happen?"

"Indeed a wild one from off the prairies," Mr. Smith agreed. "I see you know America yourself."

Gollicker grinned modestly. "Doan't let me interrupt, measter," he apologized.

Mr. Smith drew another breath. He saw he was up against at least one expert, so he made it very good. He gave them, in more senses than one, a moving picture of the cowboy's life.

When he was done, Gollicker sighed and Big Ian nodded.

"Now," Sam said, "how about them buffalo?"

"Ah, the buffalo," Mr. Smith said. "The thundering herd! The bison! For a while there was danger or thought to be—that the herds were dying out. But now, I am glad to say—and no doubt you are just as glad to hear—the herds are increasing, and ere long, again the crack of a rifle will bring down a bull in full gallop."

"But how about them Indians?" Saw put in.

Mr. Smith considered the Indians at the station in Santa Fe. They didn't seem at all satisfactory. But he was inspired. He drew himself up.

"You will pardon me if I do not speak of that," he said. "We have not too much love for the paleface who stole our lands. I say 'we,' for my mother was Yellow Blanket, a princess of the Blackfoot tribe. Therefore, let us not speak of the white man and the red man."

He stared into the fire—majestically, he hoped.

"Now, see what tha's done?" Ian said to Saw. "Happen it'll learn thee to keep thy yapper shut once in a while.... Tha maun excuse him, measter. Tell us about gangsters instead. Didta ivver run into any gangsters?"

"Run into them? Why how could you help it?" Mr. Smith asked.

Swiftly and graphically he painted for them an America in which here was the town where the bullets of the gangs crackled day and night. Here was the last street, and on it the last house, and beyond that was the trackless prairie where the buffalo thundered, the cowboy rode and the Indian ever lurked.

As he finished, he looked up. Everyone in the inn was listening. At the bar, the maid leaned on her elbows, entranced.

"Ah, I talk too much," Mr. Smith said.

"Nay, goa on, lad," they said. "Goa on."

"Well, it's dry work. How about a drink?"

"Champion," said Saw.

"Owd on," Big Ian said. "Us'll play darts for a round."

"Now, Ian, if the lad wants to buy—"

"Ah said," Ian repeated, "us'll play darts—onybody that wishes to be in on t' round. And t' loser will pay."

Mr. Smith paid anyhow, for the dart game was trickier than he had thought, and they all seemed to be experts.

He was getting very much better when the barmaid called: "Time, gentlemen, please."

Mr. Smith was sorry. It had been a good evening. They all said good night cheerfully. Big Ian shook him by the hand.

"Well, soa long, lad. We had a champion time. But Ah just want to say, that didn't fool me when tha were kidding us at first. Tha sees, for one thing, us goas to t' pictures and so us knaws whet America's really like. And then Ah'd allus heeard tell that all Yankees were liars."

"Yes," Mr. Smith said, regarding his conscience, "I did tell some lies."

"Aye, but Ah suppose it's a way ye Yankees hev," Ian said. "But it's all right as long as tha told us t' trewth finally."

144

When we imagine the Englishman out of his tweed suit, we tend to see him either in uniform (all those old colonial-war films) or dressed in one of several bizarre sporting outfits participating in one of several bizarre sports, such as cricket, punting, or the chase. Four of our travel humorists were kind, and courageous, enough to take a stab at either participating themselves or trying to interpret what the English do to amuse themselves. First, Art Buchwald will share with us his experience at an Eton-Harrow cricket match; then Margaret Halsey will tell us what a real fox hunt looks like from a variety of perspectives, including at the other end of a horse's hoof; Will Rogers will inform us about how to hunt grouse in Scotland; and Willard Price will show how much harder it is to punt a boat than a football (an American football, that is; to the Englishman, of course, football is soccer and soccer is what you never, never do).

Art Buchwald
Are You Sure It's Cricket? 1954

ONE OF THE MOST THRILLING EXPERIENCES you can have in Europe is attending the Eton-Harrow cricket match at Lord's. As everyone knows, Eton and Harrow are public schools, which means in England that they are private, and there is such a tradition of rivalry between them that a spectator has to be very careful while sitting in the stands—the person sitting next to him may be wearing the other school's necktie.

Although it was my first cricket match, I certainly enjoyed it. The thing that struck me most about the Harrow-Eton contest was how similar cricket is to our national game of baseball. It was almost as if I were watching the Brooklyn Dodgers and the New York Giants having a go of it at Ebbets Field. How many times have Americans said, "The Battle of the Alamo was won on the playing fields of Ebbets"?

Let's not talk about the differences, but about the similarities between cricket and baseball. First, we were amazed how the spectators at Lord's resembled the ones you see at the Brooklyn matches. Nearly all the men were wearing morning coats and gray top hats with waistcoats, and they all carried umbrellas. The women were splendidly outfitted in large straw hats and lovely flowered dresses. The men wore flowers in their lapels designating which team they were rooting for, a custom, no doubt, which they picked up from our own baseball games at home.

While cricket differs from baseball in a few ways, the spirit in which the game is played is very similar. Etonians and Harrovians are not so much interested in the result as they are in how the match is played. Was it a clean win? Did both sides have fun? Did the team make new friends out of the contest and did everyone hit and field as hard as the circumstances permitted? And so it is with Dodgerovians and Giantonians. As Mr. Leo Durocher, the ex-strategist of the New York team, pointed out many times, "It isn't who wins, but how you play the game that counts."

As in baseball, a cricket team must be spurred and booted and on the field at least ten minutes before the umpires go out. The visiting team is met and welcomed with the utmost consideration by the local captain and his team. Cricketers, like baseballers, realize their respective sports are not so much to win cups, pennants or glory as to meet men like themselves who wish to spend a relaxing day on the green, hitting and fielding the elusive white ball.

Instead of pitchers, cricket features bowlers, and instead of hitters, cricket has batsmen. But the object in both games is to hit the ball as hard as you possibly can in order to score as many runs for your team as is humanly possible. In cricket the score gets a little high sometimes, going as high as nine hundred runs a game, but when you consider that one cricket game can take two days or a test match five days, the number of runs scored doesn't seem unreasonable.

Cricket players always break for lunch and have a ten-minute recess for tea. The tea interval was undoubtedly adopted from America's seventh-inning stretch.

As in our national sport, the spectators of cricket applaud politely when someone has made a good batting or fielding play but refrain from mentioning it if anyone has the misfortune to make an error or strike out. Only on rare occasions may the spectators raise their voices. When a man scores a century, which means he has made one hundred runs and is sort of a Willie Mays, "three cheers for the occasion" are perfectly in order.

In discussing the similarities between the games one cannot overlook how the umpires resemble each other. A cricket umpire, like a baseball umpire, is the most respected man on the field and his eyesight and honesty are unquestioned by the spectators. It is this faith in umpires which probably makes both sports so popular with the players as well as the people in the stands.

Anyway, to get back to the Harrow-Eton match, it was a sitter for Harrow, which scored a decisive victory this year by nine wickets. For a while it looked as if Eton might win the day, and how they blew it is something I'll never know.

Margaret Halsey
Tally Ho! 1938

GENERAL AND MRS. BURTON CALLED for me this morning and we drove to the neighboring village of Compton Regis, where the Yeobridge Pack was meeting. Leaving the car in a narrow lane, we walked to the public square. In the center of the square about thirty people were stamping around on horseback. Nearly half were women, many of whom—including Mrs. Wadhams—rode sidesaddle. A massive wedge of skirt covered the sidesaddlers from waist to ankle and they appeared to be sticking to the horse's floating ribs by some interesting combination of centrifugal force and capillary action.

The square was solidly lined with children, shopkeepers, grooms, and retired military men who conversed in short, cryptic barks with General Burton. Against this fringe of humanity horses plunged and reared until I thought at least half the onlookers would be trampled to death. But this frightful prospect did not seem to disturb them, and they even appeared to enjoy having hoofs down their necks. Three of the huntsmen were wearing white breeches, brilliant red coats and black velvet caps. Why, in English novels, are hunting coats always mentioned as being pink? Is this one of the more flamboyant examples of British restraint? One of the Redcoats bestrode a horse which was submerged to the knees in a swirling mass of dogs. The dogs, dirty white with large black and brown spots, had ears like old pillowcases. Curiously enough, though they were never still, they kept solidly together, so that they all moved as a unit, but slowly and wiggling at the edges, like an amoeba.

The riders tightened their girths. Another Redcoat took up a collection—to pay the farmers, the General said, for any wire that got broken by the huntsmen. I said humbly that I should have thought it would be the huntsmen that got broken by the wire, but the General only answered, "Yes yes," as if I were wasting his time with trivialities.

There was a perpetual stir in the square, but nothing seemed to be going to happen, so after a few moments I ventured to ask who pays for the dogs.

"Hounds," corrected Mrs. Burton kindly.

"NEVER call them dogs," said the General.

I opened my mouth to re-phrase the question and a horse backed into it. I flung myself behind the General. "Take it *away*," I said. The General gave the horse a familiar poke in the buttocks. "Won't hurt you," he remarked casually over his shoulder. I resumed my place again. Mrs. Burton patted my arm and the General began to explain some of the fundamentals of the hunt. One of the local gentry keeps the hounds and either hunts them himself—in which case he is an M. F. H.—or pays a Master to hunt them for him. In either case, he hires in addition two or three "whips," who, like the Master, wear red coats and who take up collections and watch for the fox when he comes out of the cover. Those of the neighboring gentry who can afford to keep horses, pay an annual subscription to the owner of the pack—three pounds in Yeobridge, where the country is hilly; ten pounds in the Midland Counties, which are flat and fashionable.

At this point a big brown barrel moved into my range of vision and I looked up and saw two forefeet and a flushed Mammoth Cave of a mouth suspended in the air directly over my head. "Killed in a hunting accident," I thought, while the horse pawed at my temples. "It will make a nice high-class obituary." I had a momentary flash of a smiling red-faced man twenty feet above me who did not seem to know or care that he was about to indulge in manslaughter. Then the horse shrewdly realized that he could not climb a tree, because there was no tree there, and he came resignedly back to his normal posture—clearing my cheek in the process by an eighth of an inch.

"You were saying...?" I remarked faintly to the General, and Mrs. Burton looked at me proudly.

Further explanations were prevented by a great clatter of hoofs as the Master swept out of the square on a carpet of hounds, and the field rattled after him. We followed on foot. In less than three minutes the field was out of sight. This made the whole business seem pointless, but the General is not one to be interested in girlish misgivings, so I said nothing. At the edge of the village we came to a hill which I estimated roughly to be three miles high and which rose at an angle of ninety degrees. The General pointed to the top. "Ought to be able to see from there," he said. I looked at him to see if he were joking and found that he was already fifty feet ahead of me. We climbed. The road was six inches deep in mud and would have given pause to a drunken marine in a caterpillar tractor. A fine rain began to fall.

"Hey," I called to the General. "It's raining."

"Good thing," he said, looking back. "Keeps the scent down."

By the time we reached the summit my legs felt like a mess of spaghetti, but the grass was soaking wet and there was no place to sit down. Below us in the valley the field waited at some distance from the cover, while the Master and the whips patrolled the edges. A chorus of mellow howls arose from the woods. "They've found the scent," said Mrs. Burton. I was surprised at the melodiousness of the sound. In the ordinary way, it would not occur to me to look for madrigals from fifty dogs in a state of expectant agitation, but the noise that came up from the valley had a musical tenor quality and was like the clamor of bells.

We had a long wait. The rain continued with unassuming persistence and in a little while we all looked like something that had gotten tangled up in a paddle wheel.

Anyone coming along, at that point, with a cup of coffee and a sandwich could have had me drudging for him for the rest of my life. The General said that since it was the first meet of the year, the fox was probably a young one which had never been hunted before and did not know that he was supposed to run. After several seasons a fox grows so polite that he turns around and says "Yoo-hoo" to the pack whenever they lose the scent, but in his first season he is apt to be a little gauche.

The Master and one of the whips were conferring and in a minute or two the whip rode into the woods, apparently to slip the fox a note from the Rules Committee. Whatever he meant to do, he did it successfully, for the next moment three foxes burst out of the cover. The peaceful little valley boiled like a battle scene. One of the foxes tore across the fields and nearly knocked down two small boys who were standing in a public footpath surveying the proceedings. The boys screamed lustily. The second fox raced toward a neighboring farm, and all the farm people (who had been watching the hunt) started scrambling up haylofts and trees and chimneys trying to see where he went and howling "Tallyho!" (presumably) with every second breath. The third fugitive whizzed past the Master and went up toward the brow of the hill opposite us, the hounds pelting after him. The Master roared out an infuriated "Tallyho!" and blew maniacally on a little horn. But the field had deserted him. Some of them had started riding down the little boys and the rest charged the farm and were nearly out of sight before they realized the hounds were not with them.

The General was writhing. "Sheep!" he agonized. And the Master's fox was indeed flickering up the hill, headed for a flock of sheep, the hounds after him, the Master after the hounds, and the rest of the field belatedly spurring toward the bottom of the hill. The fox flashed through the sheep and I lost track of him. The hounds stopped short when they got to the sheep and began snuffing fruitlessly around like a man trying to find a stamp in a hurry when his wife is away. "It spoils the scent," Mrs. Burton said, "if he runs through sheep." The field surged up the hill. Suddenly the hounds picked up the trail again. They gave tongue and were off over the crest of the hill, the riders after them.

"May as well go home," said the General sadly. "Can't see anything more."

It seemed to me an anticlimactic end to the business, but I was glad to call it a day. I was so thoroughly wet that I almost flowed down the hill and I wondered if I would have to keep on going till I reached my own level.

"What happens," I asked the General, "when the hounds catch up with the fox?" Mrs. Burton looked disturbed and then glanced at her husband to see if he had noticed. But the General was still wistfully trying to see over the brow of the hill where the hunt had disappeared.

"Tear 'im to pieces," he answered absently. "In a minute. Messy business. Rather."

"They really are a nuisance," Mrs. Burton put in, in her soft voice. "Foxes. They do a lot of damage. And they can run very fast," she added hopefully. "Quite often they get away."

After tea this afternoon I went out to get some cigarettes. I met Mrs. Wadhams riding slowly home from the meet. It was raining hard. She was as splashed with mud as if she had gone ten rounds with an avalanche. When she nodded to me, a pint of water rolled out of the brim of her hard hat and plumped into her lap.

"Did you get him?" I asked.

"He ran over ploughed fields. Spoils the scent," she explained, and laughed. "Had a jolly good run, though." She paced sedately off through the downpour. "Glorious," she said over her shoulder.

Will Rogers
Grousicide 1926

WELL, ALL I KNOW IS just what I read in the Papers and what I see as I prowl around. It's the open season over here now in Europe for Grouse and Americans, but they shoot the Grouse and put them out of their misery. Everybody over here goes up in Scotland for what they call the shooting season. The King has gone and that means that everybody must go, even if they won't get any nearer the King than they do a Grouse, why they will go just the same. It's a great thing to rent Castles up there. Of course you can rent a Cottage or a Tent, but the class of Grouse that fly by it is really of very low grade. They have no breeding. But if you have a Castle, why then the elite among the Grouse come by there.

The way they work it is they have Scotchmen that go and drive the Birds by. That is they do it for a fee. Harry Lauder has the contract to furnish the Scotchmen. Now you get a nice, big, easy, comfortable chair and sit out in front of the Castle, and as they drive them by you shoot at them. If you don't hit any, why the Scotchmen, for an EXTRA fee, will drive the Birds into the Barronial Hall of the Castle and there you can take a few shots at 'em in there. It is great exercise, this Grouse shooting. That is, it is for the Drivers. Now in case you can't hit a Grouse, if it's too small, why they will drive you up a deer, and you can either shoot it or pet it, which ever you like. A day's shooting all depends on how good the Drivers are. If you will bring them by close enough, say up about two gun barrels length away, why you can sometimes get enough for supper. But otherwise the Scotchmen may have to kill some with a stick for supper. The whole industry is sponsored by the Ammunition Companies.

153

Now the Birds know they are going to be killed, and you would think they knew better than to fly by where the shooters are. But the way they do it, is have the Scotchmen take the Scotch Bagpipes down in the brush with them and play the pipes, and when the Birds hear the Bagpipes they will fly right into the mouth of a gun purposely. Anything to keep from hearing the Bagpipes. When they are killed the Bird coroner can always bring in a verdict of "Justifiable Homicide." The whole wonder to me is there is not more Scotchmen shot. I think they put cotton in the Hunters' ears.

Willard Price
Perils of the Punt 1958

WE HAD SAILED THE WORLD'S WATERS in almost every sort of craft but this was our first experience with an English punt. Before starting out, we asked the boat-house attendant for a few points on punts. Most important—the pole: how should it be used?

"If you've never used a pole," he said grimly, "my advice to you is to leave it severely alone."

"But there always has to be a first time."

"Yes, but aren't you beginning rather late?"

I ducked that one and examined the pole. It was as long as four men placed end to end and seemed about as heavy. It terminated in a metal prong.

"You stand in the stern," the man said. "If you try to work it from the bow, the after part of the boat will wag back and forth like the tail of a dog—or go around in circles."

"Do you operate it over the middle of the stern, or at the side?"

"At the side."

"Changing sides when necessary?"

"If you swing the pole across the boat from one side to the other you are quite likely to knock your passenger's head off. You keep it on one side and press in or out on it to steer the boat."

That was reassuring, for it was just what you did with a paddle. This was probably even easier than paddling. I comforted myself with the reflection that poling was a primitive art practised by untaught savages for thousands of years before the use of the paddle was learned.

"Let's get along," I said, and we got along, but used only the paddle until we were through the bridge and out of sight of the boat-house man. Then I laid down that light, lithe and beloved implement and took up the twenty-foot pole.

The upper end of it promptly snagged a willow tree and the punt all but passed on without us before it was extricated. By this time the punt had turned about and was headed back through the bridge.

"This tub has no keel," I said. "It spins like a top."

"Quick, do something," my wife advised me. "He'll see you with that pole."

Since this was something that obviously must not happen, I pronged a pier of the bridge and swung the boat back under the willow.

Then I tried to reach bottom with the pole. The bottom was only some ten feet down and the pole was twenty feet long, so this should have been easy. However, when the pole was thrust into the water at an angle its wooden buoyancy promptly lifted it to the surface and no amount of pressure could get it to the bottom. It was necessary to thrust it straight down.

This I did with a mighty thrust—with the result that it went deep into the muddy bottom and stuck there. I heaved and strained to get it out. In the meantime the punt was going on. There was a grave decision to be made. Should I stay with the punt or with the pole? The stretch between them was getting dangerously long. I decided on the boat and let the pole go, then paddled the boat back to retrieve it.

"Better stick to the paddle," my wife suggested. But my blood was up now. The pole and I were going to fight this out if it took all summer.

For a while it was simple. The wind was accommodating and pushed us along rapidly in the right direction. I had only to go through the motions of manipulating the pole, which actually never touched bottom. It was very easy and perhaps even graceful. A girl walking along the towpath with her man stopped and gripped his arm.

"You see, Henry," she said, "that's the way it's done."

As we said in our introduction, this is a book exclusively about England, not Scotland, Northern Ireland, or Wales. With two exceptions: Will Rogers' short piece on grouse-hunting and the following story by English travel writer H. V. Morton about his attempt on the highest peak in the British Isles: Mount Snowdon in Wales. In most countries, except Great Britain and Holland, one of the tourist's favorite forms of entertainment is climbing up and around on mountains. Yes, England's Lake District is full of nice little—well, I suppose some would call them mountains, and they are mighty steep, but.... No, there really aren't any mountains, any real mountains in England, so we'll have to sneak across the border into Wales. Anyhow, it's a good story.

H. V. Morton
A Grand Day for Snowdon 1932

YOU MAY THINK THIS IS RATHER a silly story, but Welshmen who know the climate of their country will realize that it is a true one.

At six A.M. it was a heavenly morning. The sun was shining from a blue sky. All the hills were singing with their heads in the light of morning. The lake was like blue glass. The mountain burns, swollen by days of rain, gushed in their rocky beds, and it seemed that Wales had met summer. I decided to climb Snowdon. I spent a long time with maps. I decided to go through Llanberis and tackle the Old One from Pen-y-Pass and come down him another way into Beddgelert.

While I was eating breakfast, a few clouds appeared. I dressed for the ordeal, put on the right boots, took the right stick, packed the right rucksack, and, as I was leaving, I said to the hotel boots:

"It's a grand day for Snowdon!"

"Yes, indeed—perhaps," was his mysterious reply.

The Welsh, unless they know you very well, are too polite to contradict you. I now realize that this remark translated into good Scots would be:

"It isna a guid day, man—ye're mad."

It was nearly noon when I reached Llanberis.

Oh, what had happened to the morning? The sky was grey. The sun had vanished. A thin mist hid the hills.

"You will see nothing at all," said a local authority. "I should give it up."

This made me more determined than ever. So I hung about Llanberis waiting for the day to make up its mind. At the end of the village I came to a surprising little station—the kind of station you see in the window of a toyshop. A toy engine slid out of a shed and attached itself to a long, open coach. In this coach sat about fifteen men and women. One man wore a bowler hat. Most of the women were in black. They looked as though they were going to some aerial funeral.

As I stood there in the mist thinking how strange it all was, a man in uniform came up, and seeing, perhaps, that I was a mountaineer, offered to sell me a railway ticket to Snowdon.

When I tell you I revolted, I am putting it mildly! I love mountains and respect them. I am still young enough to climb them. I know what it feels like to win a summit with a beating heart and feel that you own the earth. Would I take a ticket to Snowdon? I was insulted!

The conductor told me that a gale was blowing over the mountain, that no one with an ounce of sense had climbed it, and that his train could not get to the top. He would, however, sell me a three-quarter-way ticket for eight shillings.

"And why can't you get to the top with your foul train?" I asked.

"There is the Saddle," he said. "It is very narrow, and on either side is a drop of thousands of feet, yes, indeed. We should be blown over in this wind."

"Well, when do you start?"

"We are waiting for a telephone message from the top."

"Is there a post office there?"

"Oh, yes, indeed there is."

"And an hotel?"

"Yes."

"Then give me a ticket. It's all thoroughly immoral."

So I fell.

I took a seat right in the front of the Snowdon express, where the conductor works the brakes. Behind me was a glass partition, and the coach in which sat the saddened tourists.

As soon as I was committed to this sinful journey I became happy. Most of all, I loved to think of the hearty men with whom I have climbed mountains: Whipcord Fordie, who goes up Ben Nevis like a goat; the Pilgrim Father from Partick, who climbs solemnly; the wild doctor who sweeps through the Larig like an angry clan. How I wished these Three Musketeers could walk on the station at Llanberis and see me sitting in the train; how I would have enjoyed their horror....

A man came up the platform with the message from Snowdon. The engine, which was behind the coach, gave a startled squeal and began to push us slowly up the mountain. In half an hour we were in the clouds. Now and then, as the wind blew a hole in them, we looked down on many miles of green valley and stone walls. We puffed on over the narrow rail and it became colder. The wind waited for us round corners and came at us like a charge of cavalry.

The mourners in the coach behind were now suffering great discomfort. Some of them lay full length on the seats to escape the wind. Two women tried to let down the canvas flaps. This stopped the train. The conductor got out and warned them that if the flaps were down we might blow over if we got to the Saddle.

As we mounted, the clouds were blown straight up at us from below. It was one of those days on a mountain when you find shelter and stay near the path. The wind began to reach gale force. A man who sat next to me and had not said one word bellowed in my ear:

"It's a verra unfortunate day...."

"What part of Scotland?" I shouted at him.

"Stirling," he yelled.

"What are you doing here?"

"Having ma holidays," he shrieked.

At this point the train stopped. We could see nothing on either hand. The wind was terrible. We could feel that train shaking gently. It was icy cold. The conductor held a consultation with the engine-driver and announced that we must turn back.

"Nonsense, man!" shouted the Scotsman. "Get on wi' ye...."

"I have been here for over thirty years, look you," said the conductor, "and it is not safe to cross the Saddle today."

I got out to look at the Saddle, but I could hardly stand. Into the mist stretched a track perhaps ten or twelve feet wide, and on either side was a sheer drop of several thousand feet.

When I got back the Scotsman was still trying to persuade the train to go on to the top! But no; the conductor said that the train always played for safety first, and he would never cross the Saddle in a gale while he was in charge of it!

"I've no' had ma money's worth," said the Scotsman; then he shouted at me, "and we can get a drink at the top."

However, to the relief of the tourists, we reversed and started back. One old lady, utterly unmoved, sat with folded hands, her spectacles glistening with condensed cloud, exactly as if she were at home in a parlour at Wolverhampton.

As we slid back to earth the clouds thinned. The sun was trying to shine. We looked up and saw a mighty cloud over Snowdon. All the devils that haunt great mountains were going mad up there. I conceived a great respect for Snowdon—though I felt none for myself! I swore that I would climb it on a better day....

We stamped about Llanberis Station trying to get warm. The conductor told us that a sudden storm had swept up from the west. The Scotsman was still unsatisfied.

"Man," he said to me, "did ye pay eight shillings for yon ticket?"

"I did."

"Ye should hae got a reduced one like mine," he said, and went off happily.

Shopping in London is shopping at its best, but it's shopping—like home, but with a little bit better service, unless you go over for the after-Christmas sales. Shopping in the small towns and villages is another thing completely, even if it is being rapidly invaded by chainstores. Here is the experience of one of the most delightful travelers ever to pick up a pen, Emily Kimbrough, in trying to buy supplies for her houseboat in the town of Stone, Staffordshire, not far from the untouristed sister cities of Stoke-on-Trent and Newcastle-under-Lyme. Shopping there was, at least for us, highly amusing.

Emily Kimbrough
Shopping in Stone 1958

THERE IS NO FANTASY ABOUT SHOPPING in Stone. Shopping there, we were to find, is like shopping in any of the other English towns in which we bought provisions, but provides no kinship with any town at home. The British common denominator is inconvenience. We Americans are pampered housekeepers, pushing a cart through a supermarket and dropping into it breakfast food, vegetables, milk and butter, meat or fish, Kleenex and cigarettes. When we have checked off every item on our shopping list we pause at a counter, pay for what we have bought, see it all put into a beautiful, stout paper container and carried to our car. It is not like that in England, my dears. Staples are in one shop but nothing is provided there in which to put them.

"Have you no container?" the first shopkeeper we visited inquired incredulously and then I knew why every woman we passed carried suspended over one arm a long, limp band of woven string with handles. We admitted apologetically we had no container.

The British have patience far beyond the quota in the temperament of other people! I do not know whether this is an inherent quality, or developed by trials and an accustomedness to the inadequacy of things, and of Americans. The shopkeeper was patient with us. He wrapped our purchases in bits of paper he had saved from packages delivered to him. He had no string, and soon after we had left him our parcels began to open. A light breeze blew the flapping ends of mine across the lower part of my face in tantalizing fashion, causing me agonizedly to want to sneeze.

Each of us bought a string bag at the first shop that carried them, though this was not the first shop we visited. Nothing we required was in the first shop at which we made inquiries, and no matter which side of the street we tried first, what we needed was across the way. A busy way, crowded with trucks, "lorries" I was already saying, passenger cars, bicycles, motor bikes and other women shoppers like us, except most of these pushed a pram and herded three or four toddling stragglers.

Butter and eggs are under one roof but milk and cream are not there, any more than lettuce is to be purchased where salt and vinegar are for sale. Olive oil is purchased at the chemist's. Of course, bread is not at any of these places. It is at the baker's though there are adventurers among these who will include cakes and pastries. Meat, of course, is at the butcher's. "But whatever would make you think," that gentleman inquired benevolently, "that we would have chicken? Chicken is poultry, across the way and up the street." I had not wanted chicken nor anything else that required so much attention. On a cruise there would be views I would prefer to the inside of an oven or broiler, but I was curious to learn how far this subdivision of supplies was stretched. Also I wanted an excuse to stand still for a few minutes. For an hour we had been trudging this zigzag shopping course. My legs ached and, because I had shifted the bag from one to the other, both arms were numb. Butter, bread, milk, eggs, cheese, salt, pepper, sugar, coffee, tea. It was a list that at home could have been filled in a quarter of an hour within an area of a hundred or so paces. We were on our second hour and had made at least three laps around the course on this trial-and-error run.

Our major error had been an idea—mine—that we could purchase an ice bucket, the sort of receptacle on every cocktail tray across America. That was as moonstruck a flight of fancy as ever entered an addled pate. In the first shop where I made my naïve inquiry I met total lack of comprehension and a mistrustful scrutiny that backed me out of the door again in a hurry to rejoin Sophy. Sophy will solicit any information as long as the solicitation can be made in writing. If it must be ascertained verbally she invariably remains on the sidewalk.

Following directions from the next shopkeeper I visited, we found the goal suggested was an establishment that sold pottery. I was shown vases, bowls and platters. I dare say, to this merchant my suggestion of preserving ice was as idiotic as his was to me of a tasteful arrangement of cubes in one of the vases as a table decoration. To ask where I could buy an ice bucket had been my first mistake. To think I knew where one could be bought was my second. My third was to inquire where I might find a hardware store.

In the opinion of the shopkeepers I had already visited I was an eccentric. This was obvious in the manner of their response, soothing but wary. My use of the phrase "hardware store," a phrase made up of English words but, to their ears, heterogeneously assembled and without any meaning, provoked such a mistrustful silence from the personnel of the bakery that with a silly smile and a sickly apology, I do not know for what, I again rejoined Sophy on the sidewalk. I had no solace from her, but I had not expected it. Next to asking people questions face to face, Sophy dislikes being halted in the swift completion of her appointed rounds. I like punctuation in my prose and my activities, Sophy prefers to go straight through to the period at the end of the sentence or errand. She considered an ice bucket an interruption. Furthermore she was embarrassed, she said, by the way people inside watched me leave the shop. It was apparent to her even on the street side of the window, they considered me outlandish. She regretted being associated with me under their observation. She counted their appraisal of me justifiable, considering, she said, most English people have very little use for ice in the first place, so why would they want to keep it? She added a suggestion that since I was so quick to take on an English accent I might do well to learn an English vocabulary and not throw about such foreign phrases as "hardware store."

I had agreed to give up the search and the phrase but the butcher was so patient with my ignorance of where poultry was to be found I ventured one more try. Across Sophy's look of astonished outrage as one who has been betrayed, I asked that kind man if he could suggest a place where we might find a receptacle in which ice might be preserved. This was a new technique. I did not say "ice bucket" nor "hardware store." Furthermore I anticipated his appraisal by identifying myself—out of kindness or intimidation I did not include Sophy—as an American with a foolish eccentricity of liking cold drinks. I shook my head deprecatingly at my own folly. I thought he was going to pat my head as he leaned over the counter toward me, and Sophy jumped aside nervously. But his large red hand reached beyond my face and pointed toward the street. "Have ye tried the iron-monger's across the way?" he asked.

In the Midlands they say "noo" and I heard myself say it. "Noo," I answered, "I halven't and I thank ye very much."

"Oh my God" was what I heard Sophy mutter.

When I was a child in Muncie, Indiana, a ragged and dirty old man used to drive a wagon past our house about once a week. Over the top was strung a row of bells that jangled. Above this noise the driver called frequently, "Old iron, old iron."

Until this moment I had thought that man and others like him were ironmongers and it would not have occurred to me to rummage for an ice bucket in the contents of their wagons.

The merchandise in the establishment of the ironmonger in Stone was even more heterogeneous than the assortment I had glimpsed over the rim of the traveling carts in Muncie, though it was of a vastly superior quality. Nevertheless it did not include an ice bucket. The shop owner was sympathetic and obliging. He brought out a number of objects he thought might do, blowing dust off each one before setting it on the counter before us. The dustiest of all was a small thermos bottle that took him some time to discover. He hadn't seen it, he said, "in donkey's years," and conveyed to us his bewilderment at having stocked it in the first place. Brimming, it might have held two cups of liquid, but the neck was too small to allow the insertion of any but crushed ice. He had been so willing, however, and so uncritical of my eccentricity I could not bear to leave without making a purchase. That is why Sophy and I returned to the inn swinging between us a large pail of plastic in bright yellow.

*"We brought over some snaps of little old
London Bridge which we guessed you folks
would be dying to see."*

Siggs

&Tourists

&*Nothing in England is more humorous than the tourist. He, she, and it (the children) fit all the requirements for humor: incongruity, absurdity, pretension, ignorance, and the usual sort of bumbling good nature we love to see in films about absent-minded professors (sometimes the nature's not so good, but that's no fun!). Here are four looks at the American tourist in England, three of them by English writers, who have the best perspective on our foibles: W. H. Hudson, who as a naturalist as well as a novelist had a keen eye for the species* Tourist americanis; *H. V. Morton, who had as keen an eye as any travel writer; and W. Somerset Maugham, one of the best storytellers ever. But first an American, H. Allen Smith, looks at as ridiculous an American as he could find: himself.*

H. Allen Smith
That English Look 1952

NELLE IS COMPLAINING AGAIN about my refusal to visit such institutions as Westminster Abbey and the Tower, but I am adamant, telling her that my concern is with people, living people, and that she may feel free to indulge in that sort of rubbernecking if she chooses. Privately I don't mind confiding to my journal that my actual motive is this: I do not hanker to be identified as a barbarian American tourist. I believe that when I walk briskly through the streets I am taken for a purebred Englishman. I have noticed that people stare at me and smile, admiringly I suppose; on such occasions I sometimes deliberately drag my upper lip back, exposing my teeth, and then move my head about with little jerks as if I didn't quite know where I was, and this evokes a pleasing sensation—the feeling that one *belongs*. An attractive lady journalist named Miss Shanks called today and I mentioned the fact that Londoners seem to stare at me on the streets and she said, "It's your bow tie. Identifies you as an American. Almost nobody wears a bow tie in London, except Americans." The young lady clearly lacks perception.

W. H. Hudson
Two Ways to Visit Salisbury 1922

STROLLING ABOUT THE GREEN with this thought in my mind, I began to pay attention to the movements of a man who was manifestly there with the same object as myself—to look at the cathedral. I had seen him there for quite half an hour, and now began to be amused at the emphatic manner in which he displayed his interest in the building. He walked up and down the entire length and would then back away a distance of a hundred yards from the walls and stare up at the spire, then slowly approach, still gazing up, until coming to a stop when, quite near the wall, he would remain with his eyes still fixed aloft, the back of his head almost resting on his back between his shoulders. His hat somehow kept on his head, but his attitude reminded me of a saying of the Arabs who, to give an idea of the height of a great rock or other tall object, say that to look up at it causes your turban to fall off. The Americans, when they were chewers of tobacco, had a different expression; they said that to look up at so tall a thing caused the tobacco juice to run down your throat.

His appearance when I approached him interested me too. His skin was the color of old brown leather and he had a big arched nose, clear light blue very shrewd eyes, and a big fringe or hedge of ragged white beard under his chin; and he was dressed in a new suit of rough dark brown tweeds, evidently home-made. When I spoke to him, saying something about the cathedral, he joyfully responded in broadest Scotch. It was, he said, the first English cathedral he had ever seen and he had never seen anything made by man to equal it in beauty. He had come, he told me, straight from his home and birthplace, a small village in the north of Scotland, shut out from the world by great hills where the heather grew knee-deep. He had never been in England before, and had come directly to Salisbury on a visit to a relation.

"Well," I said, "now you have looked at it outside come in with me and see the interior."

But he refused: it was enough for one day to see the outside of such a building: he wanted no more just then. To-morrow would be soon enough to see it inside; it would be the Sabbath and he would go and worship there.

"Are you an Anglican?" I asked.

He replied that there were no Anglicans in his village. They had two Churches—the Church of Scotland and the Free Church.

"And what," said I, "will your minister say to your going to worship in a cathedral? We have all denominations here in Salisbury, and you will perhaps find a Presbyterian place to worship in."

"Now it's strange your saying that!" he returned, with a dry little laugh. "I've just had a letter from him the morning and he writes on this varra subject. 'Let me advise you,' he tells me in the letter, 'to attend the service in

Salisbury Cathedral. Nae doot,' he says, 'there are many things in it you'll disapprove of, but not everything perhaps, and I'd like ye to go.'"

I was a little sorry for him next day when we had an ordination service, very long, complicated, and, I should imagine, exceedingly difficult to follow by a wild Presbyterian from the hills. He probably disapproved of most of it, but I greatly admired him for refusing to see anything more of the cathedral than the outside on the first day. His method was better than that of an American (from Indiana, he told me) I met the following day at the hotel. He gave two hours and a half, including attendance at the morning service, to the cathedral, inside and out, then rushed off for an hour at Stonehenge, fourteen miles away, on a hired bicycle. I advised him to take another day—I did not want to frighten him by saying a week— and he replied that that would make him miss Winchester. After cycling back from Stonehenge he would catch a train to Winchester and get there in time to have some minutes in the cathedral before the doors closed. He was due in London next morning. He had already missed Durham Cathedral in the north through getting interested in and wasting too much time over some place when he was going there. Again, he had missed Exeter Cathedral in the south, and it would be a little too bad to miss Winchester too!

H. V. Morton
Saxophones in Heaven 1935

HE WAS STANDING IN THE CATHEDRAL Close at Exeter, reading his guide book like a good American, ready to be friendly on the slightest provocation....

I was thinking that if you close your mind to detail, the cathedral cities of England are deliciously alike—they have grown up on the same pattern out of the same past. I like the invariable narrow entrance to the precincts; the green trees which look as if each one is valeted; the close-cut grass; the bright chatter of sparrows; the slow chime of bells; the discreet Georgian doors with heavy brass knockers which mark themselves out as the barriers between the world and the dean's dignity. Each close is drenched in the same air of ancient peace; high above dream the gray walls and towers, whose every stone proclaims an age of boundless faith....

The American entered Exeter Cathedral, and I followed.

Here is a piece of perfectly balanced architecture—a beautiful, but, to me, unemotional cathedral; each arch the exact echo of another arch, each pillar the replica of its opposite. It is like a problem in mathematics set to music. It is almost too perfect! At one moment it seems that the whole fragment might fly up to heaven or dissolve in cold, formal music. The thing that keeps Exeter Cathedral firmly rooted to earth is the organ erected in an unfortunate position above the choir, so that you cannot see beyond to the great east window. This is Exeter's anchor of ugliness!

I know that it is a marvelous organ; that because Exeter is the one cathedral in England with transeptal towers there is no other place for it. That does not lessen the shock.

"Can you tell me what a recorder is?" said the American.

"A magistrate."

"No; it's some kind of musical instrument. This book says that the angels carved on the minstrels' gallery are playing a viol, a harp, bag-pipes, a trumpet, an organ, cymbals, and—a recorder!"

We went up together and looked at the earliest English stone orchestra I know of.

"That's a recorder!" I suggested. "That instrument played by the third angel from the left."

"Gee! That's a kind of old English saxophone."

"It *is* rather like a saxophone!"

"Well, that's pretty good; saxophones in heaven!"

We walked out into the close, talking. He had "stopped off" the "boat" at Plymouth, and was, as he put it, "just tickled to death" by Exeter.

"I don't know a thing about England yet," he said, "but I'm getting a line on her. If it's all like this—well, I'm right glad I came over!"

I asked him what "tickled" him about Exeter.

He replied thoughtfully: "D'you know America?"

"I regret to say I have never been there."

"Well, we kind of sneer at tradition, but, believe me, under our skins we admire it and wish we had it. We don't know what it is to have roots. Now this morning I went to a whale of a place, the City Hall here—the Guildhall they call it—that old place with a top story hanging over the main street. There's an official there called a sergeant-at-mace. He told me things about this town till I was dizzy. You've had a lot of kings in England! That fellow talked familiarly about William the Con- queror, King Charles, and a queen called—wait while I look at my diary—Henrietta, and then he took me upstairs, and showed me the mayor's chains and things. Proud as Lucifer he was, because something or other was older than something or other in London! And I saw a sword covered in old black cloth. I said to him, just to see his reaction, 'Why don't you get all that stuff off it; what's the idea?' He looked at me shocked. I could see him thinking: 'You poor ignorant fish!' 'That sword, sir,' he said, 'was put in mourning for King Charles the First, and it's still in mourning for him!' Well, gee, I just walked right out..."

"The motto in this town is 'always faithful'!"

"Sure! History means a lot. I can imagine what it feels like to have a city like Exeter in the family. I'm a New Englander, so I guess I've got English blood in me, and maybe that's why an old town like this thrills me. Now look at this crazy old shop!"

We went into a bookshop, where I bought a map of Cornwall.

"I don't know," said the bookseller shyly, "whether you two gentlemen would care to step upstairs and see my old room."

We went up a dark staircase, and entered a low room that overhung the High Street. The floor was uneven, the ceiling was Stuart, the walls were paneled in oak, the windows were small and leaded.

"Prince Rupert lived here when Exeter was held for the king!"

"Well, what do you think of that?" said the American.

We went down again.

"I don't know who Prince Rupert was," whispered my friend, "but—that was just grand! Good-by! What gets me is that sword! Can you beat it?"

Somerset Maugham
The Wash Tub 1936

POSITANO STANDS on the side of a steep hill, a disarray of huddled white houses, their tiled roofs washed pale by the suns of a hundred years; but unlike many of these Italian towns perched out of harm's way on a rocky eminence it does not offer you at one delightful glance all it has to give. It has quaint streets that zigzag up the hill and battered, painted houses in the baroque style, but very late, in which Neapolitan noblemen led for a season lives of penurious grandeur. It is indeed almost excessively picturesque and in winter its two or three modest hotels are crowded with painters, male and female, who in their different ways acknowledge by their daily labours the emotion it has excited in them. Some take infinite pains to place on canvas every window and every tile their peering eyes can discover and doubtless achieve the satisfaction that rewards honest industry. "At all events it's sincere," they say modestly when they show you their work. Some, rugged and dashing, in a fine frenzy attack their canvas with a pallet knife charged with a wad of paint, and they say: "You see, what I was trying to bring out was my personality." They slightly close their eyes and tentatively murmur: "I think it's rather me, don't you?" And there are some who give you highly entertaining arrangements of spheres and cubes and mutter sombrely: "That's how I see it!" These for the most part are strong silent men who waste no words.

But Positano looks full south and the chances are that in summer you will have it to yourself. The hotel is clean and cool and there is a terrace, overhung with vines, where you can sit at night and look at the sea bespangled with dim stars. Down at the Marina, on the quay, is a little tavern where you can dine under an archway off anchovies and ham, macaroni and fresh-caught mullet, and drink cold wine. Once a day the steamer from Naples comes in, bringing the mail, and for a quarter of an hour gives the beach (there is no port and the passengers are landed in small boats) an air of animation.

One August, tiring of Capri where I had been staying, I made up my mind to spend a few days at Positano, so I hired a fishing-boat and rowed over. I stopped on the way in a shady cove to bathe and lunch and sleep, and did not arrive till evening. I strolled up the hill, my two bags following me on the heads of two sturdy women, to the hotel, and was surprised to learn that I was not its only guest. The waiter, whose name was Giuseppe, was an old friend of mine, and at that season he was boots, porter, chambermaid and cook as well. He told me that an American *signore* had been staying there for three months.

"Is he a painter or a writer or something?" I asked.

"No, *signore*, he's a gentleman."

Odd, I thought. No foreigners came to Positano at that time of year but German Wandervögel, looking hot and dusty, with satchels on their backs; and they only stayed overnight. I could not imagine anyone wishing to spend three months there; unless of course he was hiding. And since all London had been excited by the flight earlier in the year of an eminent, but dishonest, financier, the amusing thought occurred to me that this mysterious stranger was perhaps he. I knew him slightly and trusted that my sudden arrival would not disconcert him.

"You'll see the *signore* at the Marina," said Giuseppe, as I was setting out to go down again. "He always dines there."

He was certainly not there when I arrived. I asked what there was for dinner and drank an americano, which is by no means a bad substitute for a cocktail. In a few minutes, however, a man walked in who could be no other than my fellow-guest at the hotel and I had a moment's disappointment when I saw that he was not the absconding financier. A tall, elderly man, bronzed after his summer on the Mediterranean, with a handsome, thin face. He wore a very neat, even smart, suit of cream-coloured silk and no hat. His gray hair was cut very short, but was still thick. There was ease in his bearing, and elegance. He looked round the half-dozen tables under the archway at which the natives of the place were playing cards or dominoes and his eyes rested on me. They smiled pleasantly. He came up.

"I hear you have just arrived at the hotel. Giuseppe suggested that as he couldn't come down here to effect an introduction you wouldn't mind if I introduced myself. Would it bore you to dine with a total stranger?"

"Of course not. Sit down."

He turned to the maid who was laying a cover for me and in beautiful Italian told her that I would eat with him. He looked at my americano.

"I have got them to stock a little gin and French vermouth for me. Would you allow me to mix you a very dry martini?"

"Without hesitation."

"It gives an exotic note to the surroundings which brings out the local colour."

He certainly made a very good cocktail and with added appetite we ate the ham and anchovies with which our dinner began. My host had a pleasant humour and his fluent conversation was agreeable.

"You must forgive me if I talk too much," he said presently. "This is the first chance I've had to speak English for three months. I don't suppose you will stay here long and I mean to make the most of it."

"Three months is a long time to stay at Positano."

"I've hired a boat and I bathe and fish. I read a great deal. I have a good many books here and if there's anything I can lend you I shall be very glad."

"I think I have enough reading matter. But I should love to look at what you have. It's always fun looking at other people's books."

He gave me a sharp look and his eyes twinkled.

"It also tells you a good deal about them," he murmured.

When we finished dinner we went on talking. The stranger was well read and interested in a diversity of topics. He spoke with so much knowledge of painting that I wondered if he was an art critic or a dealer. But then it appeared that he had been reading Suetonius and I came to the conclusion that he was a college professor. I asked him his name.

"Barnaby," he answered.

"That's a name that has recently acquired an amazing celebrity."

"Oh, how so?"

"Have you never heard of the celebrated Mrs Barnaby? She's a compatriot of yours."

"I admit that I've seen her name in the papers rather frequently of late. Do you know her?"

"Yes, quite well. She gave the grandest parties all last season and I went to them whenever she asked me. Everyone did. She's an astounding woman. She came to London to do the season, and, by George, she did it. She just swept everything before her."

"I understand she's very rich?"

"Fabulously, I believe, but it's not that that has made her success. Plenty of American women have money. Mrs Barnaby has got where she has by sheer force of character. She never pretends to be anything but what she is. She's natural. She's priceless. You know her history, of course?"

My friend smiled.

"Mrs Barnaby may be a great celebrity in London, but to the best of my belief, in America she is almost inconceivably unknown."

I smiled also, but within me; I could well imagine how shocked this distinguished and cultured man would be by the rollicking humour, the frankness, with its tang of the soil, and the rich and vital experience of the amazing Mrs Barnaby.

"Well, I'll tell you about her. Her husband appears to be a very rough diamond; he's a great hulking fellow, she says, who could fell a steer with his fist. He's known in Arizona as One-bullet Mike."

"Good gracious. Why?"

"Well, years ago in the old days he killed two men with a single shot. She says he's handier with his gun even now than any man West of the Rockies. He's a miner, but he's been a cowpuncher, a gunrunner and God knows what in his day."

"A thoroughly Western type," said my professor, a trifle acidly I thought.

"Something of a desperado, I imagine. Mrs Barnaby's stories about him are a real treat. Of course everyone's been begging her to let him come over, but she says he'd never leave the wide-open spaces. He struck oil a year or two ago and now he's got all the money in the world. He must be a great character. I've heard her keep the whole dinner-table spellbound when she's talked of the old days when they roughed it together. It gives you quite a thrill when you see this gray-haired woman, not at all pretty, but exquisitely dressed, with the most wonderful pearls, and hear her tell how she washed the miners' clothes and cooked for the camp. Your American women have an adaptability that's really stupendous. When you see Mrs Barnaby sitting at the head of her table, perfectly at home with princes of the blood, ambassadors, cabinet ministers and the duke of this and the duke of that, it seems almost incredible that only a few years ago she was cooking the food of seventy miners."

"Can she read or write?"

"I suppose her invitations are written by her secretary, but she's by no means an ignorant woman. She told me she used to make a point of reading for an hour every night after the fellows in camp had gone to bed."

"Remarkable!"

"On the other hand One-bullet Mike only learnt to write his name when he suddenly found himself under the necessity of signing cheques."

We walked up the hill to our hotel and before separating for the night arranged to take our luncheon with us next day and row over to a cove that my friend had discovered. We spent a charming day bathing, reading, eating, sleeping and talking, and we dined together in the evening. The following morning, after breakfast on the terrace, I reminded Barnaby of his promise to show me his books.

"Come right along."

I accompanied him to his bedroom where Giuseppe, the waiter, was making his bed. The first thing I caught sight of was a photograph in a gorgeous frame of the celebrated Mrs Barnaby. My friend caught sight of it too and suddenly turned pale with anger.

"You fool, Giuseppe. Why have you taken that photograph out of my wardrobe? Why the devil did you think I put it away?"

"I didn't know, *signore*. That's why I put it back on the *signore*'s table. I thought he liked to see the portrait of his *signora*."

I was staggered.

"Is my Mrs Barnaby your wife?" I cried.

"She is."

"Good lord, are you One-bullet Mike?"

"Do I look it?"

I began to laugh.

"I'm bound to say you don't."

I glanced at his hands. He smiled grimly and held them out.

"No, sir, I have never felled a steer with my naked fist."

For a moment we stared at one another in silence.

"She'll never forgive me," he moaned. "She wanted me to take a false name, and when I wouldn't she was quite vexed with me. She said it wasn't safe. I said it was bad enough to hide myself in Positano for three months, but I'd be damned if I'd use any other name than my own." He hesitated. "I throw myself on your mercy. I can do nothing but trust to your generosity not to disclose a secret that you have discovered by the most unlikely chance."

"I will be as silent as the grave, but honestly I don't understand. What does it all mean?"

"I am a doctor by profession and for the last thirty years my wife and I have lived in Pennsylvania. I don't know if I have struck you as a roughneck, but I venture to say that

Mrs Barnaby is one of the most cultivated women I have ever known. Then a cousin of hers died and left her a very large fortune. There's no mistake about that. My wife is a very, very rich woman. She has always read a great deal of English fiction and her one desire was to have a London season and entertain and do all the grand things she had read about in books. It was her money and although the prospect did not particularly tempt me, I was very glad that she should gratify her wish. We sailed last April. The young Duke and Duchess of Hereford happened to be on board."

"I know. It was they who first launched Mrs Barnaby. They were crazy about her. They've boomed her like an army of press agents."

"I was ill when we sailed, I had a carbuncle which confined me to my stateroom, and Mrs Barnaby was left to look after herself. Her deck chair happened to be next the duchess's and from a remark she overheard it occurred to her that the English aristocracy were not so wrapped up in our social leaders as one might have expected. My wife is a quick little woman and she remarked to me that if you had an ancestor who signed Magna Charta perhaps you were not excessively impressed because the grandfather of one of your acquaintances sold skunks and the grandfather of another ran ferry boats. My wife has a very keen sense of humour. Getting into conversation with the duchess she told her a little Western anecdote and to make it more interesting told it as having happened to herself. Its success was immediate. The duchess begged for another and my wife ventured a little further. Twenty-four hours later she had the duke and duchess eating out of her hand. She used to come down to my stateroom at intervals and tell me of her progress. In the innocence of my heart I was tickled to death and since I had nothing else to do, I sent to the library for the works of Bret Harte and primed her with effective touches."

I slapped my forehead.

"We said she was as good as Bret Harte," I cried.

"I had a grand time thinking of the consternation of my wife's friends when at the end of the voyage I appeared and we told them the truth. But I reckoned without my wife. The day before we reached Southampton Mrs Barnaby told me that the Herefords were arranging parties for her. The duchess was crazy to introduce her to all sorts of wonderful people. It was a chance in a thousand; but of course I would spoil everything; she admitted that she had been forced by the course of events to represent me as very different from what I was. I did not know that she had already transformed me into One-bullet Mike, but I had a shrewd suspicion that she had forgotten to mention that I was on board. Well, to make a long story short, she asked me to go to Paris for a week or two till she had consolidated her position. I didn't mind that. I was much more inclined to do a little work at the Sorbonne than to go to parties in Mayfair, and so, leaving her to go on to Southampton, I got off at Cherbourg. But when I had been in Paris ten days she flew over to see me. She told me that her success had exceeded her wildest dreams: it was ten times more wonderful than any of the novels; but my appearance would ruin it all. Very well, I said, I would stay in Paris. She didn't like the idea of that; she said she'd never have a moment's peace so long as I was so near and might run across someone who knew me. I suggested Vienna or Rome. They wouldn't do either, and at last I came here and here have I been hiding like a criminal for three interminable months."

"Do you mean to say you never killed the two gamblers, shooting one with your right hand and the other with your left?"

"Sir, I have never fired a pistol in my life."

"And what about the attack on your log cabin by the Mexican bandits when your wife loaded your guns for you and you stood the siege for three days till the federal troops rescued you?"

Mr Barnaby smiled grimly.

"I never heard that one. Isn't it a trifle crude?"

"Crude! It was as good as any Wild West picture."

"If I may venture a guess that is where my wife in all probability got the idea."

"But the wash tub. Washing the miners' clothes and all that. You don't know how she made us roar with that story. Why, she swam into London Society in her wash tub."

I began to laugh.

"She's made the most gorgeous fools of us all," I said.

"She's made a pretty considerable fool of me, I would have you observe," remarked Mr Barnaby.

"She's a marvellous woman and you're right to be proud of her. I always said she was priceless. She realized the passion for romance that beats in every British heart and she's given us exactly what we wanted. I wouldn't betray her for worlds."

"It's all very fine for you, sir. London may have gained a wonderful hostess, but I'm beginning to think that I have lost a perfectly good wife."

"The only place for One-bullet Mike is the great open West. My dear Mr Barnaby, there is only one course open to you now. You must continue to disappear."

"I'm very much obliged to you."

I thought he replied with a good deal of acidity.

Big Macs

*H*ave recently been making a sort of spot
check on raincoats and umbrellas. The
raincoat, or mac, is as essential to an Englishman as his teeth but actually there are not a
great many umbrellas—nothing like what we
were told in New York, where we were assured
that our very first purchase on arrival in London would necessarily be an umbrella. The raincoats do the job for almost everyone on the
streets; the umbrella is more of a badge, indicat-
ing the owner is a member of one of the profes-
sions, or the aristocracy. The proper furling of
an umbrella is regarded as an art, and lessons
are given in it by experts at the big stores. An
umbrella that has been correctly furled is such
a sleek and beautiful object that many Englishmen refuse to mess it up by opening it in a
rainstorm. We have not bought one of these implements and it looks as if we'll make it
through without one. — *H. Allen Smith, 1952*

"Say—it's really great to be invited into a typical English home."

✿Return

✿*At no time in his journey is the foreign traveler more a traveler than when he gets back home and tells people what he did. There's no doubt that one feels apart from one's surroundings when one travels in a foreign land, even if the foreigners speak a similar sort of language. But when one gets home, among his or her fellows, why he's welcomed back not as good old George or Jean, but as someone who's expected to have had exotic experiences, to tell all, and to have a good stock of photos or slides to back their stories up (at least no one expects a tan when you go to England). Knowing the expectations of our family and friends—beyond the presents, of course—we spend our return trip and, sometimes, part of our last days, readying ourselves for the ordeal we see ahead of us: making up stories, practicing accents, etc. The jet stream that flows against you coming home is God's gift to those of us who will have to suffer rather than enjoy ourselves once we land.*

Of course, there's a flip side: nothing is worse for the stay-at-home than to hear and see the newly-returned traveler who can talk of nothing else but.... Just ask the neutral, not even rhetorical question, "So what's new?" and out it spews, a flood of events and non-events, opinions and advice.

To remind those of us who choose to forget how rough the coming home of the ordinary Odysseus can be, here are Petroleum V. Nasby, Frances Douglas & Thelma Lecocq, and, for the scientific touch, Stephen Leacock, Hum.D.

Petroleum V. Nasby
All Travelers Lie 1882

ALL TRAVELERS LIE. I am going to try to be an exception to this rule, and shall, to the best of my ability, cling to the truth as a shipwrecked mariner does to a spar. I shall try to conquer the tendency to lie that overcomes every man who gets a hundred miles away from home. But I presume I shall fail; and so when I get home and say that living is cheaper and better in London than it is anywhere in America, please say to me, "You are lying!" You will do the correct thing.

No doubt when there I shall say to Smith or Thompson, "My boy, what you want to do is to go abroad. You want to see London. And as for the expense, what is it? Your passage across is only one hundred dollars—ten days—and that is but ten dollars a day. And then you can live so much cheaper in London than you can in New York that it is really cheaper to go abroad than it is to stay at home."

I presume I shall say this when I get home, for I know the tendency of the traveler to lie. I have traveled all over North America, and I confess, with shame mantling my cheek, that I have at times added some feet to the height of mountains and to the width of rivers, and to the number of Indians, and once I did invent an exploit which never happened, and I have narrated incidents which never occurred. It is such a temptation to be a hero when you know you can never be successfully disputed.

While I am yet young in foreign travel, and capable of an approximation to truth, I wish to say that London is not only not a cheap place to live, but an exceedingly dear one.

Frances Douglas & Thelma Lecocq
For the Folks Back Home 1946

TIME NOW TO BE THINKING of the folks back home. They'll expect travel to have broadened you, and you mustn't disappoint them.

If Yorkshire pudding, boiled potatoes, and spotted dog haven't done all they might in this direction (though this seems incredible), you'll have to do a little window-dressing on your own.

In laying a foundation, the best groundwork is a good set of vest and drawers, all wool and a yard wide, guaranteed not to shrink in the washing, but to become bigger and better as time goes on. Top this by a suit or costume of the best Harris tweed, preferably in a nice shade of rusty brown (this is the color they paint barns back home and the effect is not dissimilar). Add one part Scotch in the form of a Fair Isle jumper done in a pattern of many colors (in ordering, remember these come in two sizes, large and larger). A square-crowned felt, *en bash,* woollen socks or stockings, and British Brogues will complete the picture, broadly speaking. Attired thus, you may dock at New York, Montreal, Bombay, Tokio, or Civita Vecchia and rest assured that every one within scratching distance knows that if you are not actually English, you have at least been there and absorbed the atmosphere of the place.

To further give you that English air, try half a cup of lavender water behind the ears or a pint of gin poured down the gullet. Both are from the species juniper, and the fragrance is not unlike.

About now you will be expected to say something, and you must be careful. One hoot through your nose and the whole effect will be shattered. One flat 'a,' long 'o,' or terminal 'r' and you'll find your tweeds completely undone.

However, don't disturb yourself too much. Try as you will to go native, the English themselves will continue to think your accent too, too absurdly Canadian, Japanese, American, or Hottentot. But the folks back home are different. One 'bawth,' whether you actually have it or only 'rawthah' think you'll have it, will stamp you immediately as one apart. Whereas, if you can manage a 'mahvellous' or two before and after meals—a 'beastly' and a 'jolly' as you wash behind your ears—and a bit of Wooster sauce and Lester Square every now and then for piquancy, your reputation as an Anglophool is practically established. This may seem difficult at first, but wait till you've been home a while. It's a trick that grows on you as the years pass, and the farther your trip recedes into the background, the more English you'll become.

Stephen Leacock
Back from Europe
THE REACTION OF TRAVEL
ON THE HUMAN MIND 1926

THERE COMES A TIME EVERY YEAR when all the hundreds of thousands of people who have been over to Europe on a summer tour get back again. It is very generally supposed that a tour of this kind ought to have a broadening effect on the mind, and this idea is vigorously propagated by the hotel companies at Schlitz, Bitz, Biarritz, and picturesque places of that sort.

It is not for me to combat this idea. But I do know that in certain cases at least, a trip to Europe sets up a distinct disturbance of the intellect. Some of these afflictions are so well defined that they could almost be definitely classified as diseases. I will quote only a few among the many examples that might be given.

I. ARISTOCROPSIS, OR WEAKENING OF THE BRAIN FROM CONTACT WITH THE BRITISH ARISTOCRACY.

There seems to be no doubt that a sudden contact with the titled classes disturbs the nerve cells or ganglions of the traveler from America, and brings on a temporary enfeeblement of mind. It is generally harmless, especially as it is usually accompanied by an extreme optimism and an exaggerated sense of importance.

Specimen Case. Winter conversation of Mr. John W. Axman, retired hardware millionaire of Fargo, Dakota, in regard to his visit to England.

"I don't know whether I told you that I saw a good deal of the Duke of Dumpshire while I was in England. In fact, I went to see him at his seat—all these dukes have seats, you know. You can say what you like about the British aristocrats, but when you meet one like the Duke of Dumpshire, they are all right. Why, he was just as simple as you or me, or simpler. When he met me, he said, 'How are you?' Just like that.

"And then he said, 'You must be hungry. Come along and let's see if we can find some cold beef.' Just as easy as that. And then he said to a butler or someone, 'Go and see if you can find some cold beef.' And presently the butler came back and said, 'There's some cold beef on the table, Sir,' and the Duke said, 'All right, let's go and eat it.' And he went and sat right down in front of the beef and ate it. Just as you or I would.

"All the time we were eating it, the Duke was talking and laughing. He's got a great sense of humor, the Duke has. After he'd finished the beef, he said, 'Well, that was a darn good piece of beef!' and of course we both roared. The Duke's keen on politics, too—right up to date about everything. 'Let's see,' he said, 'who's your President now?' In fact, he's just as keen as mustard, and looks far ahead too. 'France,' he said to me, 'is in for a hell of a time.'"

II. NUTTOLINGUALISM, OR LOSS OF ONE'S OWN LANGUAGE AFTER THREE WEEKS ACROSS THE SEA

Specimen Case. Verbatim statement of Mr. Phin Gulch, college student from Umskegee College, Oklahoma, made immediately on his return from a three weeks athletic tour in England with Oklahoma Olympic Aggregation.

"England certainly is a ripping place. The chaps we met were simply topping. Of course here and there one met a bounder, but on the whole one was treated absolutely top hole." * * *

III. MEGALOGASTRIA, OR DESIRE TO TALK ABOUT FOOD

Specimen Case. Mr. Hefty Undercut, of Saskatoon, Saskatchewan, retired hotel man, talks on European culture.

"I don't mind admitting that the English seem to me away ahead of us. They're further on. They know how to do things better. Now you take beefsteak. They cut it half as thick again as we do, and put it right on a grid over hot coals. They keep the juice in it. Or take a mutton chop. The way they cook them over there, you can eat two pounds to one that you eat here. You see they're an older people than we are.

"Or take sausages—when I travel I like to observe everything; it makes you broader—and I've noticed their sausages are softer than ours, more flavoring to them. Or take one of those big deep meat pies—why, they eat those big pies at midnight. You can do it there. The climate's right for it.

"And, as I say, when I travel I go around noticing everything and sizing everything up—the meat, the lobsters, the kind of soup they have, everything. You see, over there there's very little sunlight and the air is heavy and you eat six times a day. It's a great place."

IV. INTROSPEXOSIS, OR SEEING IN OTHER PEOPLE WHAT IS REALLY IN YOURSELF

It appears that many people when they travel really see nothing at all except the reflection of their own ideas. They think that what they are interested in is uppermost everywhere. They might just as well stay at home and use a looking glass. Take in witness,

The evidence of Mr. Soggie Spinnage, Secretary of the Vegetarian Society of North, Central, and South America, as given after his return from a propaganda tour in England.

"Oh, there's no doubt the vegetarian movement is spreading in England. We saw it everywhere. At Plymouth a man came right up to me and he said, 'Oh, my dear Brother, I wish we had a thousand men here like you. Go back,' he said, 'go back and bring over a thousand others.' And whenever I spoke I met with such enthusiasm.

"I spoke, I remember, in Tooting-on-the-Hump—it's within half an hour of London itself. And when I looked into their dear faces and told them about the celery in Kalamazoo, Michigan, and about the big cabbages in the South Chicago mud flats, they just came flocking about me! 'Go back,' they said, 'go back and send those over.'

"I heard a man in a restaurant one day say to the waiter, 'Just fetch me a boiled cabbage. I want nothing else.' I went right up to him, and I took his hand and I said, 'Oh, my dear friend, I have come all the way from America just to hear that.' And he said, 'Go back,' he said, 'go back and tell them that you've heard it.'

"Why, when you go to England you just see vegetables, vegetables, everywhere. I hardly seemed to see anything else. They say even the King eats vegetables now. And they say the Bishop of London only eats beans. I heard someone say that the Bishop seemed full of beans all the time.

"Really I felt that the cause was just gaining and growing all the time. When I came to leave, a little group of friends come down to the steamer to say good-bye. 'Go back,' they said, 'go back and send someone else.'

"That seemed to be the feeling everywhere."

Well, it's time to say goodbye. Cheerio. Ta ta. You should be prepared now for everything England has to offer, and not disappointed in all it doesn't have (e.g., warmth, passion, and plumbing). You should be prepared to take the land by storm (a tempest in a teapot?) and stray far from the beaten track or, at the very least, enjoy the footsteps as much as the sights. Remember: when you get home you'll spend a lot more time imitating the accents than you'll ever spend remembering this nave or that painting. So open your ears as much as your eyes, and enjoy!

Islands

*E*ach [English]man walks, eats, drinks, shaves, dresses, gesticulates, and, in every manner acts and suffers without reference to the bystanders, in his own fashion, only careful not to interfere with them or annoy them; not that he is trained to neglect the eyes of his neighbors—he is really occupied with his own affair and does not think of them. Every man in this polished country consults only his convenience, as much as a solitary pioneer in Wisconsin. I know not where any personal eccentricity is so freely allowed, and no man gives himself any concern with it. An Englishman walks in a pouring rain, swinging his closed umbrella like a walking-stick; wears a wig, or a shawl, or a saddle, or stands on his head, and no remark is made. And as he has been doing this for several generations, it is now in the blood.

In short, every one of these islanders is an island himself, safe, tranquil, incommunicable.
—*Ralph Waldo Emerson, 1856.*

Acknowledgments

Cartoons by Siggs, Karel Capek, J. B. Handelsman, Hawker, Mahood and Norman Mansbridge reprinted by permission of *Punch*; *Some Good Advice, Glossary, The Scribbler's London, Why on the Left, That English Look* and *Big Macs* by H. Allen Smith by permission of Harold Matson Co. Inc.; *How it came to be the Strange Thing it is Today* and *For the Folks Back Home* by Frances Douglas & Thelma Lecocq by permission of J. M. Dent & Sons Ltd.; *Extraordinary Behaviour, Impressions of London, Train Etiquette* and *Back from Europe* by Stephen Leacock by permission of Random Century Group; *Filling in the Blanks, English Conversation, A Bumper Crop of Dead Knights, Poet Worship, The Pagan Abandon of Margate* and *Tally Ho!* by Margaret Halsey by permission of Simon and Schuster Inc.; *A Perspective Experience* by Christopher Morley by permission of Harper Collins Publishers; *Getting Around, Pleasure is Subjective* and *Simply Frightful* by Ruth McKenney & Richard Bransten by permission of Curtis Brown Ltd.; *A Harmony of its Own* by Hancock Bartov by permission of Valentine, Mitchell & Co. Ltd.; *A Visit to London* by Frank Sullivan by permission of the Historical Society of Sarasota Springs; Cartoons by Osbert Lancaster by permission of Curtis Brown Ltd.; *An Amazing Labyrinth* and *Perils of the Punt* by Willard Price by permission of Mrs Willard Price; *The Isle of London, Mayflower House, A Grand Day for Snowdon* and *Saxophones in Heaven* by H. V. Morton by permission of Octopus Publishing Group Library; *Ordeal at Ascot* and *Are you Sure it's Cricket?* by Art Buchwald by permission of the author; *What They Do* and *At Home* by Paul Theroux by permission of Aitken & Stone Ltd.; *Contradictions* by Pierre Daninos by permission of Random Century Group; *The Lion and the Unicorn* by George Santayana by permission of Constable & Co. Ltd.; *Two Sides of English Humour* by Ephraim Kishon by permission of Eric Glass Ltd.; *A Weakness for Ruins, Mightier than Stonehenge* and *The Round Table* by Charles Brooks by permission of Harcourt Brace and Jovanovich Inc.; *What we Missed* by Robert Benchley by permission of Harper Collins Publishers; *All Yankees are Liars* by Eric Knight by permission of Curtis Brown Ltd.;

Grousicide by Will Rogers by permission of the Will Rogers Memorial; *Shopping in Store* by Emily Kimbrough by permission of Harper Collins Publishers; *The Wash Tub* by W. Somerset Maugham by permission of Octopus Publishing Group Library.

The publishers have made every effort to trace the copyright holders of the material included in this volume and would offer their apologies in those cases where they have been unsuccessful.